BASIC SKILLS

Volume 2

HAL LEONARD STUDENT PIANO LIBRARY

Ear Without Fear

A Comprehensive Ear-Training Program for Musicians

TABLE OF CONTENTS

A Note to Students 3

A Note to Teachers 5

CHAPTER 1: Letter names and the treble clef 7

CHAPTER 2: Intervals (2nd, 3rd, 4th) and *so* below *do* 11

CHAPTER 3: *la* below *do*, the Bass Clef, and the Grand Staff 15

CHAPTER 4: Ledger lines, *so*, and the 5th 19

CHAPTER 5: Sharps, Half Steps, and *ti* below *do* 23

CHAPTER 6: Moveable *do*, *do* above *do*, and the Octave 27

CHAPTER 7: Flats and *fa* 32

and the 6th 37

....40

....44

ISBN 978-0-634-08800-1

HAL•LEONARD®
CORPORATION
7777 W. BLUEMOUND RD. P.O. BOX 13819 MILWAUKEE, WI 53213

Copyright © 2008 by HAL LEONARD CORPORATION
International Copyright Secured   All Rights Reserved

For all works contained herein:
copying, arranging, adapting, recording or public performance is an infringement of copyright.
Infringers are liable under the law.

Visit Hal Leonard Online at
www.halleonard.com

A Note to Students

You will find this series easy to use. To use the books effectively, you will need a pitch pipe or your instrument and a CD player.

Each chapter is divided into smaller sections. This allows you to focus on one section for a short period of time. Working in small sections is more valuable than trying to cover large amounts of material. Learning this way lays a good foundation as you continue to build your skills.

All exercises and dictations may be used repeatedly for additional practice or review. For written exercises, you may either erase your answers or use a separate sheet of paper.

YOUR CD:

- You may access tracks on your CD by moving from smaller numbers up or from larger numbers down. Simply press the track buttons to find the desired track number.
- This button will move forward through the CD.
- This button will move backward through the CD. Larger numbers may be easily reached by moving backward from Track 1 while the CD is playing.
- The dictations and exercises are played once. Repeat tracks as many times as necessary to complete each exercise.

YOUR WORKBOOK:

All of the chapters are set up in the same way. Labeled headings appear on the left-hand side of the page. These headings introduce a series of tasks designed to familiarize you with various melodic concepts and patterns.

LISTENING

Under this heading, your CD will provide exercises that will train your ear. Some examples may include exercises in which you will provide answers based on what you hear. The first one is usually done for you so all you have to do is listen. See **LISTENING** p. 8 for an example.

IDENTIFYING

This next heading provides you with exercises on the CD to listen to and new concepts to practice. You will often need to fill in the blanks, providing answers based on what you hear. See **IDENTIFYING** p. 12 for an example.

DICTATION

This heading contains a series of exercises in which you will write down the melodic patterns that you hear.

On the CD, you will hear each dictation once. Repeat the tracks as often as necessary to complete each exercise. Simply listen the first time, then complete the dictations as instructed. See **DICTATION** p. 10 for an example.

NEW ELEMENT

New musical concepts will be introduced under this heading. See **NEW ELEMENT** p. 7 for an example.

MATCHING

Under this heading, you will see a series of boxes containing melodic patterns. You will match the pattern you hear on the CD by indicating the corresponding letter in the space provided. See **MATCHING** p. 13 for an example.

SIGHT-SINGING

This heading provides an opportunity for you to sing, at first sight, a series of pitches notated on the staff. To begin each exercise, you will need to play the first pitch on your instrument or pitch pipe.

It is important to sing the exercises in a range where they sit most comfortably in your voice.

Remember, with the exercises and dictations, accuracy is what counts. Speed will come later.

You and your teacher may want to chart your progress. Keep a log showing the number of times you had to listen to the exercises before you were able to complete them, and how accurately you were able to perform the sight-singing exercises the first time through. See **SIGHT-SINGING** p. 9 for an example.

INTEGRATION

Exercises under this heading introduce a rhythmic component, added to help develop well-rounded listening skills. It is important to begin to hear not only melodic movement, but to hear rhythmic patterns as well. See **INTEGRATION** p. 31 for an example.

We recommend that you use the companion series:

Rhythm Without the Blues

Rhythm Without the Blues is a comprehensive rhythm-training program. Using these two series together will help you to master the dictations and exercises in Volumes 3, 4, and 5 with success.

A Note to Teachers

Ear Without Fear is an innovative program aimed at building a foundation for reading music and developing the skills to perform it accurately.

Ear training demands heightened listening skills that involve hearing and understanding pitch differentiation. Ear training is distinct from rhythm, which is mathematical in structure and employs different neurological pathways. Because both elements are invariably placed together in music training, the result is often frustration and a sense of failure. In this series, these elements are ultimately combined. Volumes 2, 3, 4, and 5 provide exercises that integrate melodic and rhythmic components.

Educators have long known that step-by-step learning is essential. A sense of accomplishment and confidence at each level is the motivating force behind the desire to continue. This series offers demonstrations, listening exercises, sight-singing, and melodic dictations which will help students to reinforce and hone melodic skills.

We have carefully chosen and organized the materials in this book to make the learning process as accessible to students as possible. The Workbook and the CDs are integrated to provide several learning approaches: AURAL, VISUAL, and PRACTICAL. Together, they present a comprehensive, step-by-step learning program for which the student can assume primary responsibility.

The following concepts will be covered in Volume 2:

- introduction to letter names and ledger lines
- introduction to treble and bass clefs
- introduction to sharps and flats
- introduction to moveable do
- introduction to intervals: 2nd, 3rd, 4th, 5th, 6th, and octave
- demonstrations, exercises, and dictations covering the above areas.

These materials make use of the tonic sol-fa music reading system developed by British educator John Curwen (1816–1880). Tonic sol-fa facilitates pitch recognition and differentiation.

Here is why teachers are finding this series an invaluable aid in the studio and classroom:

- It provides a prepared curriculum.
- Students can work independently with well-formatted, easily understood exercises.
- Chapters are easily subdivided for appropriately-sized weekly assignments.
- Exercises and dictations are readily available for weekly testing and instruction.
- Lesson time is maximized for instrumental instruction, while ensuring that the student is honing musicianship skills.

Students often find the development of essential rhythm and ear-training skills less exciting than learning an instrument, so a reward system may be helpful. Consider implementing one, using some of the following suggestions:

- Encourage students to keep a log outlining the number of sections and exercises completed over the week. They may also want to keep track of how long it takes to complete each exercise. Students' confidence will grow as they begin to see an increase in proficiency and speed.

- Award incentive points for successful completion of sections and increased proficiency. Give prizes and awards based on accumulated points.

It is recommended that students also use the companion series:

Rhythm Without the Blues

Rhythm Without the Blues is a comprehensive rhythm-training program that works in tandem with *Ear Without Fear*. Using them together will greatly enhance the ability of the student to master successfully the dictations and exercises contained in each series.

CHAPTER 1

Letter names and the treble clef

As we learned in *Ear Without Fear Volume 1*, pitches are notated on a staff. The lines and spaces on the staff are also identified using the MUSICAL ALPHABET. Letter names are helpful when we need to indicate specific pitches on the staff.

The musical alphabet uses the first seven letters of the alphabet: A B C D E F G.

Do, *re*, and *mi* in the following examples can also be called G, A, and B.

NEW ELEMENT

G is on the second line from the bottom of the staff

A is in the second space

B is on the third line

The treble clef is also known as the G CLEF. In the next example, you can see that the lower loop in the treble clef encircles the G line. The shape of this clef evolved from the letter "G" and is now a stylized version of that letter. The TREBLE STAFF has the treble clef placed on it and is used to notate high pitches.

To draw the treble clef, first write a "J" with a large dot at the end.

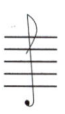

Then add a "D" that extends above the staff and down to the fourth line.

Continue with a "C" curving down to the first line.

Finish with an incomplete circle around the G line.

Use the staves provided to practice drawing treble clefs.

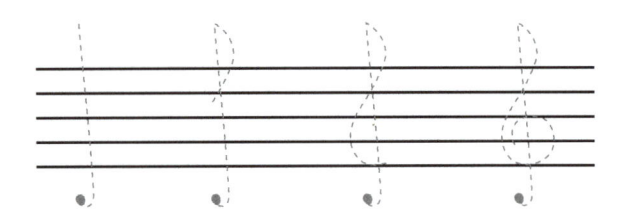

LISTENING

Exercise A is written out for you. Using it as a guide, complete the remaining exercises. Remember to fill in the directional shorthand first, then the tonic sol-fa, letter names, and the notes. Answers are on page 44.

PLAY CD TRACKS 1–4

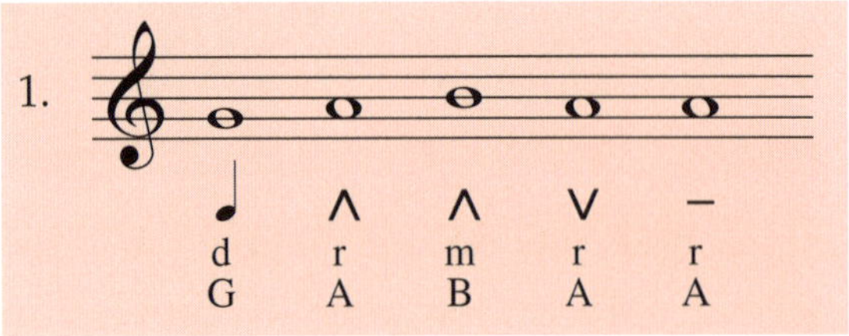

1.
	∧	∧	∨	—
d	r	m	r	r
G	A	B	A	A

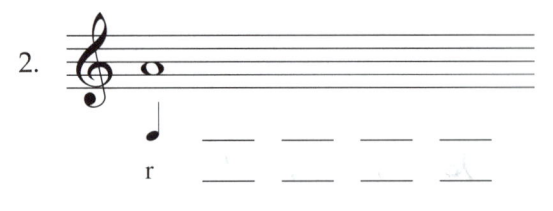

2. r

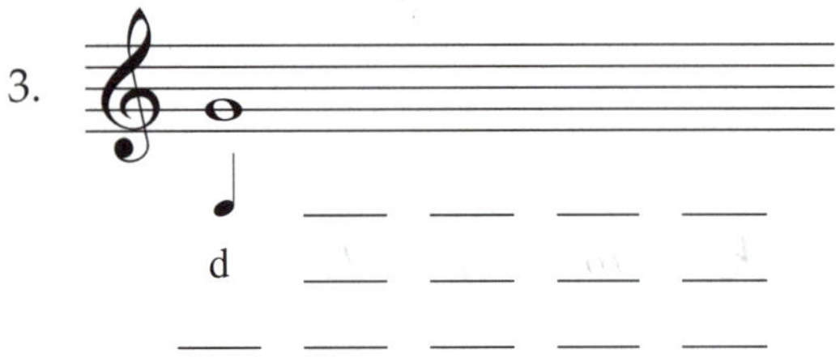

3. d

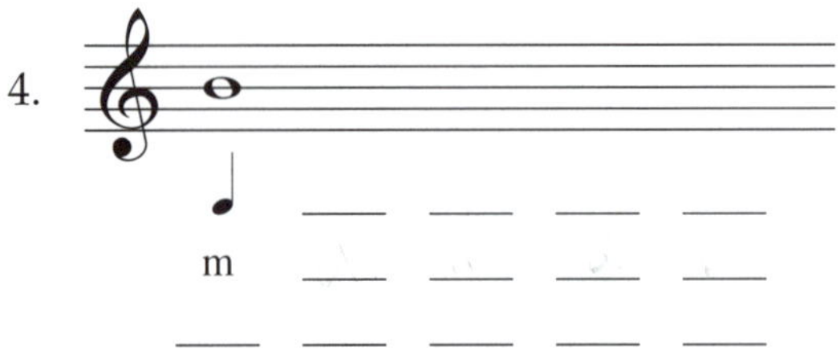

4. m

MATCHING

Listen to Track 5, which will play six different melodies, and find the matching melody. Write the letter of the matching box in the space provided. Repeat the track if necessary. Answers are on page 44.

PLAY CD TRACK 5

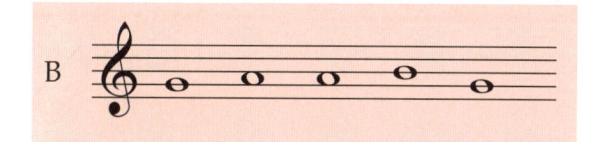

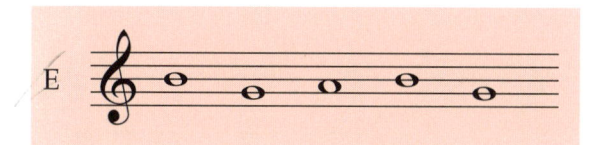

A [staff with notes]   B [staff with notes]

C [staff with notes]   D [staff with notes]

E [staff with notes]   F [staff with notes]

1. _____   2. _____   3. _____

4. _____   5. _____   6. _____

SIGHT-SINGING

For each of the following exercises, play the initial pitch on your instrument or pitch pipe. For example, the letter B is written under the first note of Exercise 1. This means to sound a B to establish the starting pitch. Sing each exercise twice, once using tonic sol-fa and once using letter names. Check for accuracy on your instrument or pitch pipe.

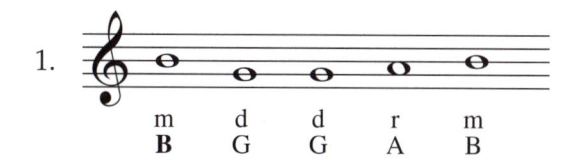

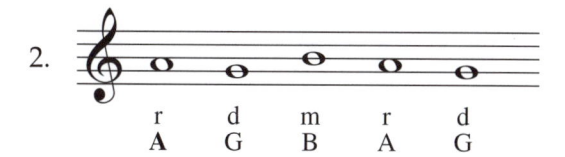

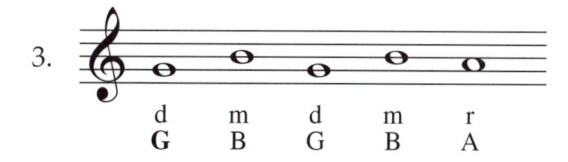

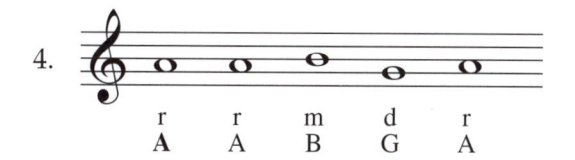

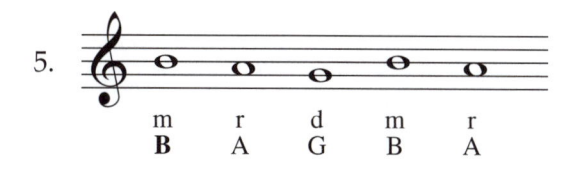

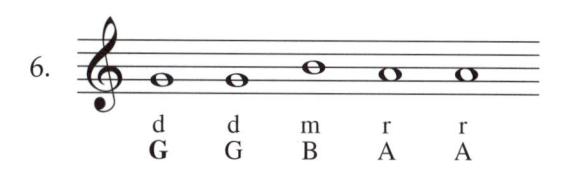

1.
m d d r m
B G G A B

2.
r d m r d
A G B A G

3.
d m d m r
G B G B A

4.
r r m d r
A A B G A

5.
m r d m r
B A G B A

6.
d d m r r
G G B A A

9

DICTATION

Play the tracks one at a time. Each track will play the melody twice. Write the melodic pattern that you hear. The starting pitch is given. Fill in the directional shorthand first, followed by the letter names, then the notes. Repeat the track if necessary. Answers are on page 44.

PLAY CD TRACKS 6–11

1. G _ _ _ _ _

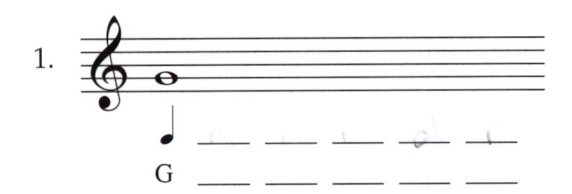

2. B _ _ _ _ _

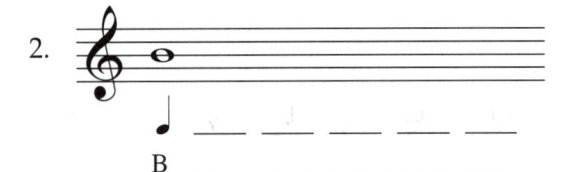

3. A _ _ _ _ _

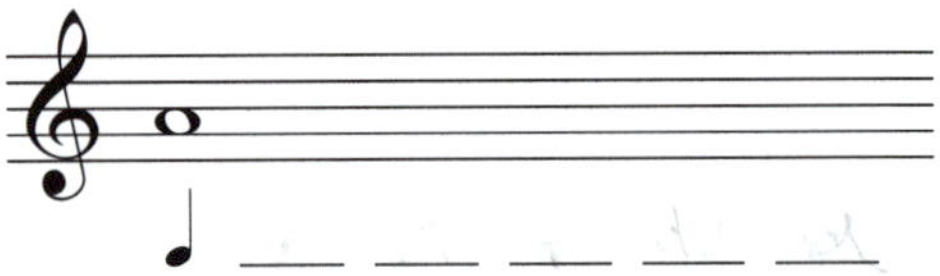

4. A _ _ _ _ _

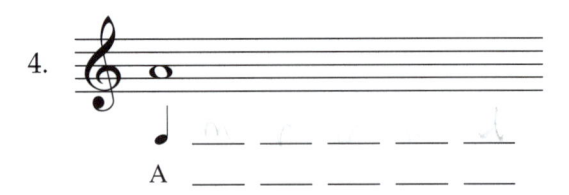

5. G _ _ _ _ _

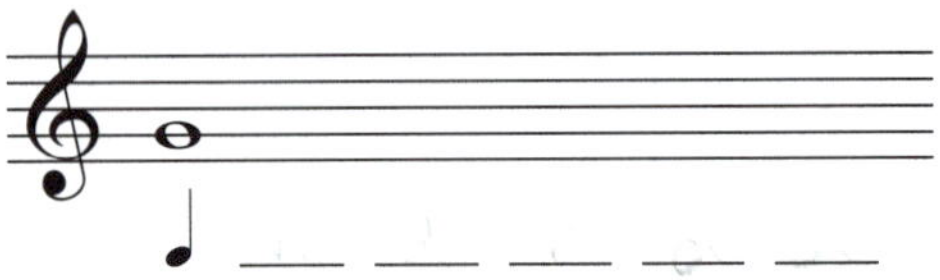

6. B _ _ _ _ _

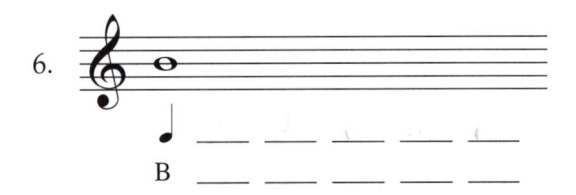

CHAPTER 2

Intervals (2nd, 3rd, 4th) and *so* below *do*

An **INTERVAL** is the distance between two notes (pitches). The distance is determined by counting the number of lines and spaces from one note to the next. In the following example, the notes are a step apart: A to B. Start by counting the A space as 1 and the B line as 2. This interval is called a **2nd**.

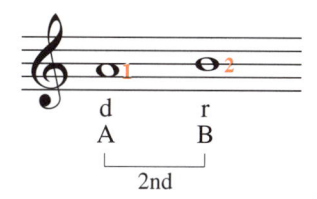

In the next example, the notes are a skip apart: G to B. We start by counting the G line as 1, the A space as 2, and finally the B line as 3. This interval is called a **3rd**.

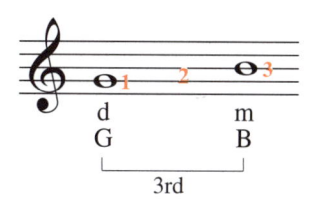

LISTENING

Listen for the 3rd in this children's tune "Looby Loo."

PLAY CD TRACK 12

IDENTIFYING

Listen and identify the intervals in the following exercises as either up or down a 2nd or a 3rd, and then write in the notes. The first one has been done for you. Answers are on page 44.

PLAY CD TRACK 13

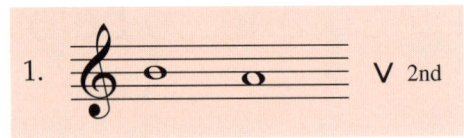

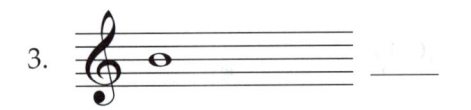

1. ∨ 2nd
2.
3.
4.
5.

NEW ELEMENT

Our new note is *so*. It is written in the space below the bottom line of the staff. The letter name for this pitch is D. The lower index symbol "ı" is used to the right of the tonic sol-fa name to indicate pitches below *do*.

Tonic Sol-fa Shorthand

s_1 = so

s₁
D

The interval from G to D is called a **4th**.

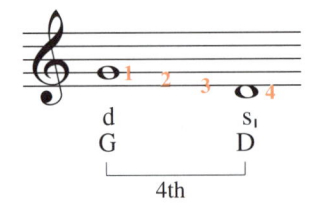

d   s₁
G   D
  4th

LISTENING

Listen for the 4th in the "Bridal Chorus" from the opera *Lohengrin* by German composer Richard Wagner (1813–1883).

PLAY CD TRACK 14

Sometimes it is helpful to use a familiar tune to help you remember and identify intervals. For example, using the first two pitches of Wagner's "Bridal Chorus" will help you remember and identify the interval of a 4th.

IDENTIFYING

Listen and identify the intervals in the following exercises as either up or down a 2nd, 3rd, or 4th, and then write in the notes. The first one has been done for you. Answers are on page 44.

PLAY CD TRACK 15

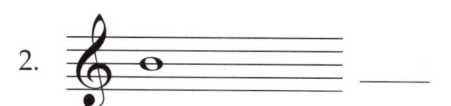

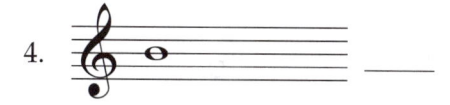

1. V 2nd
2.
3.
4.

MATCHING

Listen to Track 16 and find the matching melodies below. Write the letter of the matching melody in the space provided. Answers are on page 44.

PLAY CD TRACK 16

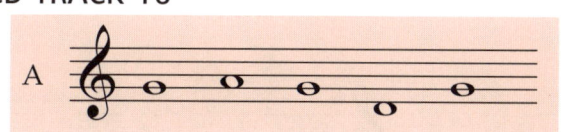

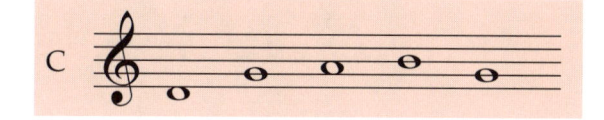

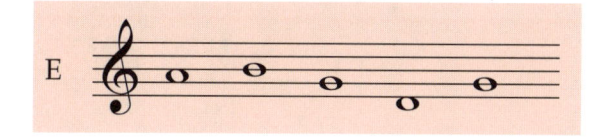

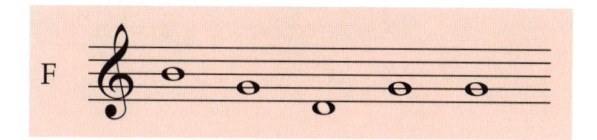

A B
C D
E F

1. _____   2. _____   3. _____
4. _____   5. _____   6. _____

13

SIGHT-SINGING

For each of the following exercises, play the initial pitch on your instrument or pitch pipe. Sing each exercise twice, once using tonic sol-fa and once using letter names. Check for accuracy on your instrument or pitch pipe.

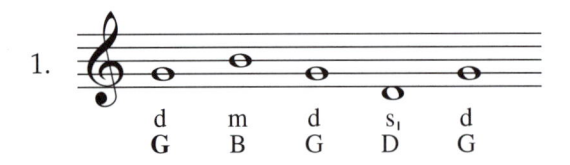

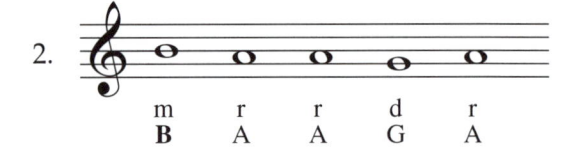

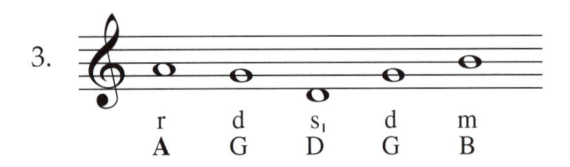

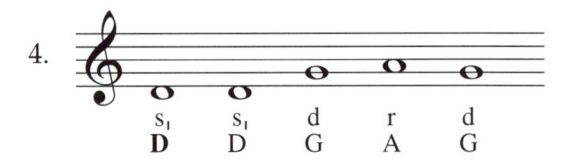

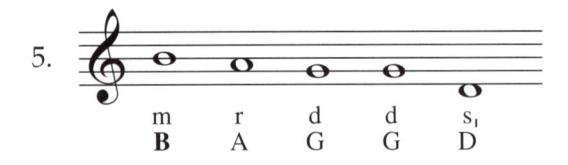

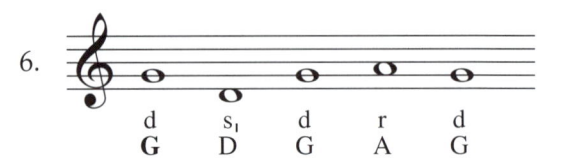

1.
d	m	d	s,	d
G	**B**	**G**	**D**	**G**

2.
m	r	r	d	r
B	**A**	**A**	**G**	**A**

3.
r	d	s,	d	m
A	**G**	**D**	**G**	**B**

4.
s,	s,	d	r	d
D	**D**	**G**	**A**	**G**

5.
m	r	d	d	s,
B	**A**	**G**	**G**	**D**

6.
d	s,	d	r	d
G	**D**	**G**	**A**	**G**

DICTATION

Play the tracks one at a time. Each track will play the melody twice. Write the melodic pattern that you hear. Answers are on page 44.

PLAY CD TRACKS 17–22

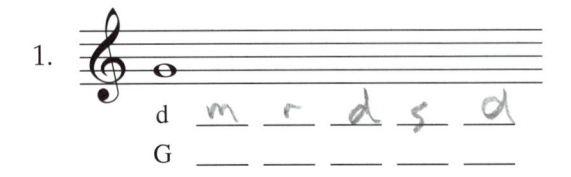

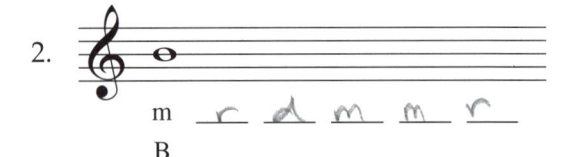

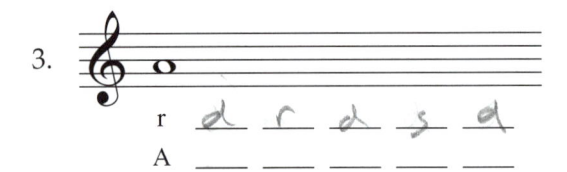

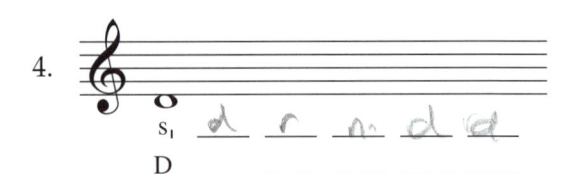

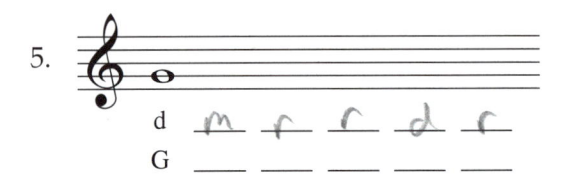

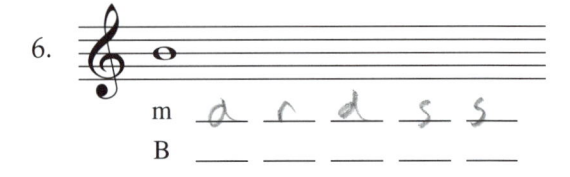

1. d _m_ _r_ _d_ _s_ _d_
   G ___ ___ ___ ___ ___

2. m _r_ _d_ _m_ _m_ _r_
   B ___ ___ ___ ___ ___

3. r _d_ _r_ _d_ _s_ _d_
   A ___ ___ ___ ___ ___

4. s, _d_ _r_ _m_ _d_ _d_
   D ___ ___ ___ ___ ___

5. d _m_ _r_ _d_ _r_
   G ___ ___ ___ ___ ___

6. m _d_ _r_ _d_ _s_ _s_
   B ___ ___ ___ ___ ___

CHAPTER 3
la below do, the Bass Clef, and the Grand Staff

NEW ELEMENT

Our new note is *la* below *do* and is written on the first line of the staff. The letter name for this pitch is E.

Tonic Sol-fa Shorthand
l₁ = *la* below *do*

l₁
E

The interval from G to E is called a **3rd**.

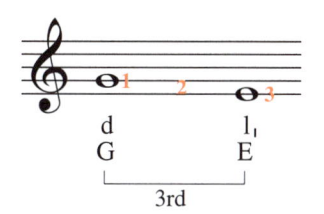

d   l₁
G   E
3rd

LISTENING

Listen for the 3rd below in the children's chant "Rain, Rain Go Away."

PLAY CD TRACK 23

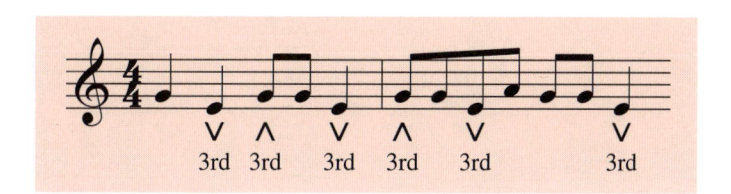

V   ∧   V   ∧   V   V
3rd 3rd 3rd 3rd 3rd   3rd

Remember: Familiar tunes such as the one given in our example can help with interval identification.

IDENTIFYING

Listen and identify the intervals in the following exercises as either up or down a 2nd, 3rd, or a 4th, then write in the notes. The first one has been done for you. Answers are on page 45.

15

PLAY CD TRACK 24

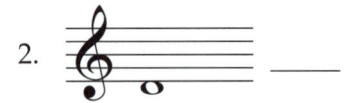

1. ∨ 3rd   2. ____

3. ____   4. ____

MATCHING

Listen to Track 25 and find the matching melodies below. Write the letter of the matching melody in the space provided. Answers are on page 45.

PLAY CD TRACK 25

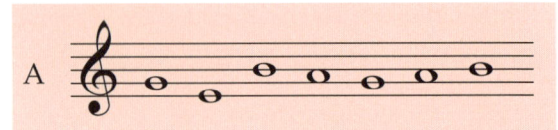

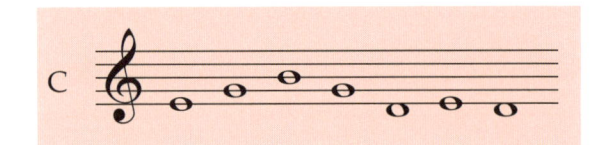

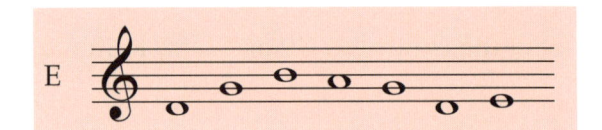

A   B

C   D

E   F

1. ____   2. ____   3. ____

4. ____   5. ____   6. ____

SIGHT-SINGING

For each of the following exercises, play the initial pitch on your instrument or pitch pipe. Sing each exercise twice, once using tonic sol-fa and once using letter names. Check for accuracy on your instrument or pitch pipe.

1.
d m r d l, s, d
G B A G E D G

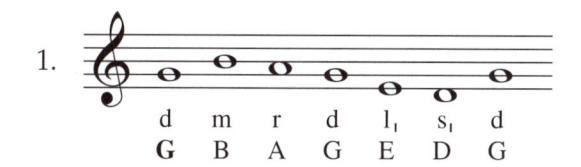

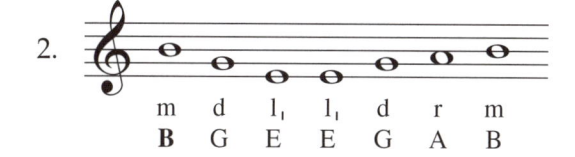

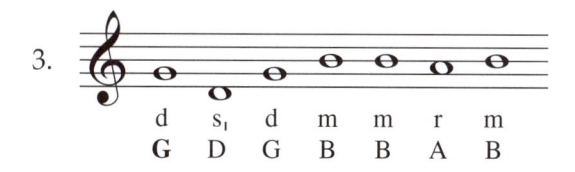

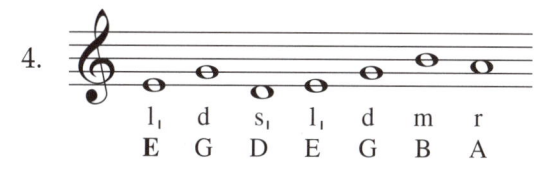

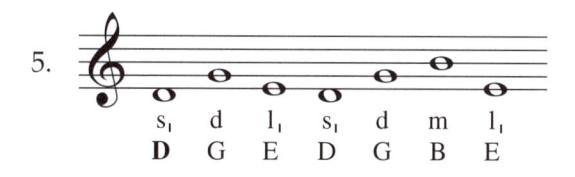

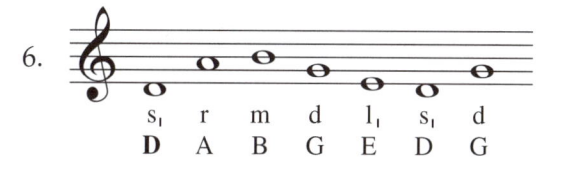

2.
m d l, l, d r m
B G E E G A B

3.
d s, d m m r m
G D G B B A B

4.
l, d s, l, d m r
E G D E G B A

5.
s, d l, s, d m l,
D G E D G B E

6.
s, r m d l, s, d
D A B G E D G

DICTATION

Play the tracks one at a time. Each track will play the melody twice. Write the melodic pattern that you hear. Answers are on page 45.

PLAY CD TRACKS 26–31

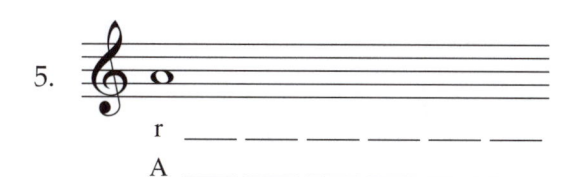

1.
d ___ ___ ___ ___ ___ ___
G ___ ___ ___ ___ ___ ___

2.
s, ___ ___ ___ ___ ___ ___
D ___ ___ ___ ___ ___ ___

3.
l, ___ ___ ___ ___ ___ ___
E ___ ___ ___ ___ ___ ___

4.
m ___ ___ ___ ___ ___ ___
B ___ ___ ___ ___ ___ ___

5.
r ___ ___ ___ ___ ___ ___
A ___ ___ ___ ___ ___ ___

6.
l, ___ ___ ___ ___ ___ ___
E ___ ___ ___ ___ ___ ___

In Volume 1, Chapter 6, we were introduced to the treble clef. We have been using it in all our examples and exercises.

This chapter provides an introduction to the **BASS CLEF**. The bass clef is also known as the **F Clef**.

Here is a bass staff:

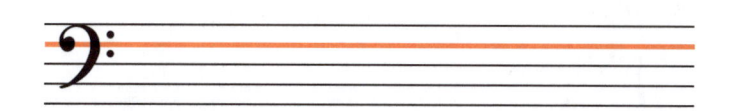

In the previous example, you can see that the two dots are placed on either side of the F line. The shape of this clef evolved from the letter F, and is now a stylized version of this letter. The bass staff is used to notate low pitches.

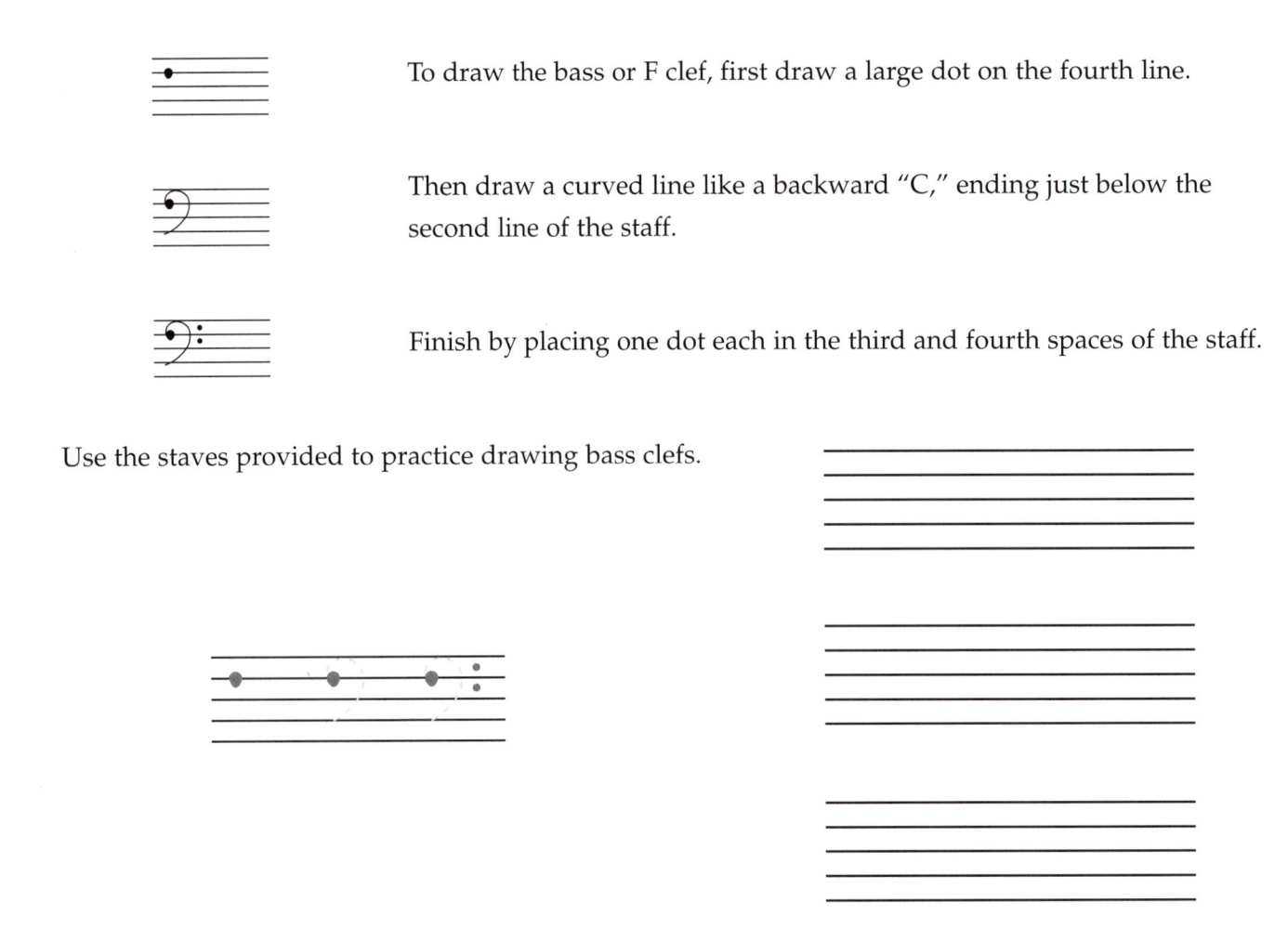

To draw the bass or F clef, first draw a large dot on the fourth line.

Then draw a curved line like a backward "C," ending just below the second line of the staff.

Finish by placing one dot each in the third and fourth spaces of the staff.

Use the staves provided to practice drawing bass clefs.

We know that notes written on the lines and in the spaces indicate the pitches. Let's look at where *do*, *re*, and *mi* will be when the bass clef appears at the beginning of the staff.

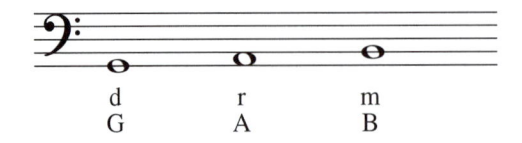

d r m
G A B

To demonstrate how the treble staff and the bass staff fit together, study the figure below. You will notice that the two staves are joined together by a **BRACE** (or bracket). When the two staves are joined in this way, it is called the **GRAND STAFF**. The pitches written on the treble staff are higher than the pitches written on the bass staff.

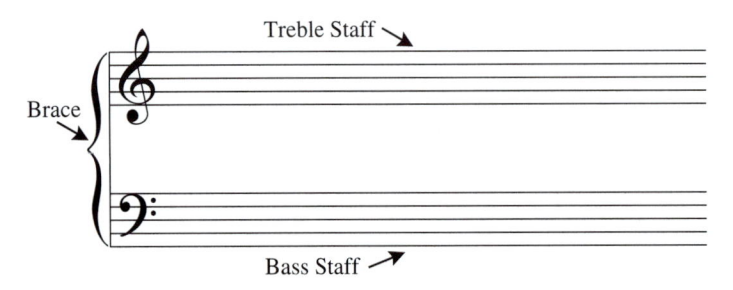

Brace
Treble Staff
Bass Staff

CHAPTER 4

Ledger lines, *so*, and the 5th

In our last chapter, we studied the bass staff and the grand staff. Sometimes the pitches are lower or higher than a staff allows. To extend the staff, short lines called **LEDGER LINES** may be added above or below each staff. In the illustration below, two ledger lines have been added above the treble staff and below the bass staff. However, as many lines as needed may be used to make the necessary notations for any given piece of music. The names of these lines and spaces follow the order of the musical alphabet.

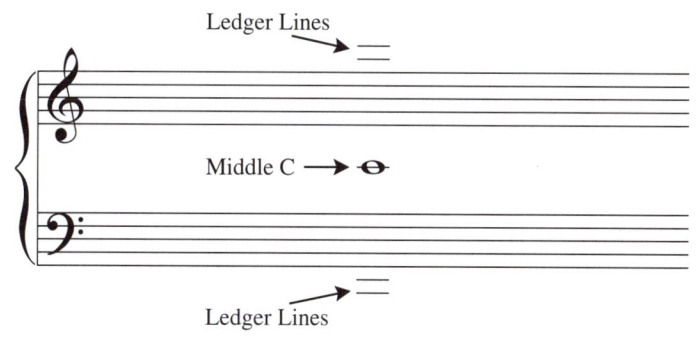

Study the example below. *Do* to *la* and *do* to *so*, in the treble clef, do not require the use of ledger lines. However, to show *do* to *la* and *do* to *so* in the bass clef, ledger lines must be used.

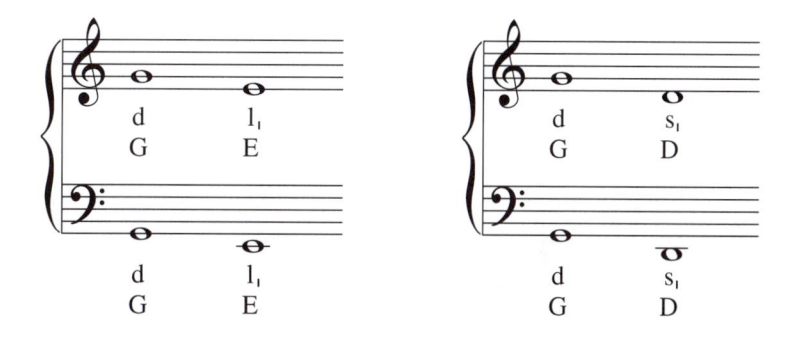

The name of the first ledger line below the bass staff is E, and the space underneath it is called D.

NEW ELEMENT

Our new interval is the *so* above *do*. The letter name for this pitch is D. It is written on the fourth line of the treble staff and the third line of the bass staff.

Tonic Sol-fa Shorthand

s = *so* above *do*

s
D

s
D

The interval from G to D is called a **5th**.

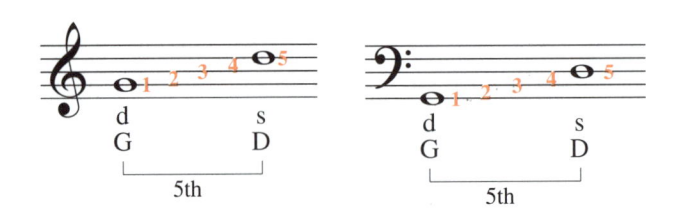

d   s
G   D
└─5th─┘

d   s
G   D
└─5th─┘

LISTENING

Listen for the 5th above in "Twinkle, Twinkle, Little Star."

PLAY CD TRACK 32

∧
5th

Singing the first interval of "Twinkle, Twinkle, Little Star"
will help you identify the interval of a 5th.

IDENTIFYING

Listen and identify the intervals in the following exercises as either up or down a 2nd, 3rd, 4th, or 5th, then write in the notes. The first one has been done for you. Answers are on page 45.

PLAY CD TRACK 33

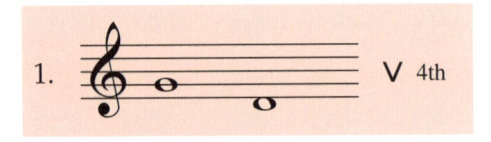

1. ∨ 4th

2.

3.

4.

5.

6.

MATCHING

Listen to Track 34 and find the matching melodies below. Write the letter of the matching melody in the space provided. Answers are on page 45.

PLAY CD TRACK 34

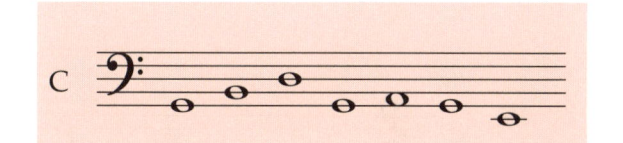

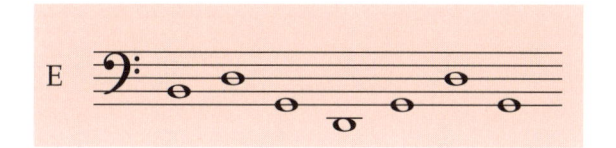

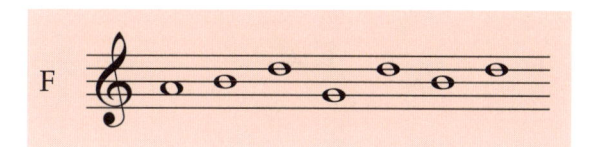

A

B

C

D

E

F

1. _____ 2. _____ 3. _____

4. _____ 5. _____ 6. _____

SIGHT-SINGING

Sing each exercise twice, once using tonic sol-fa, and once using letter names. Check for accuracy on your instrument or pitch pipe.

Remember, it is important to sing the exercises where they sit most comfortably in your voice.

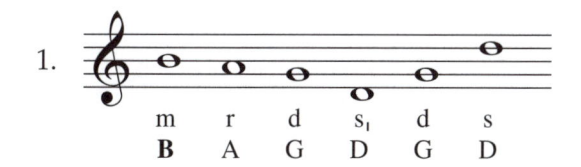

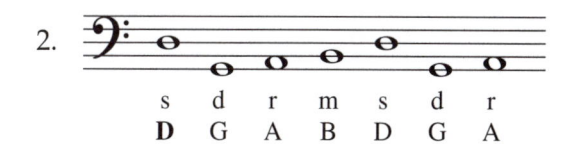

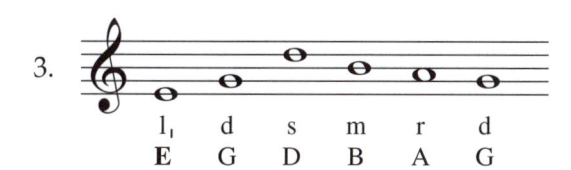

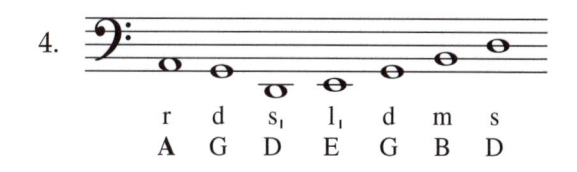

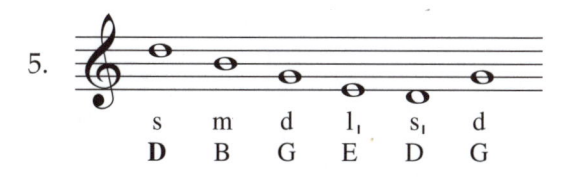

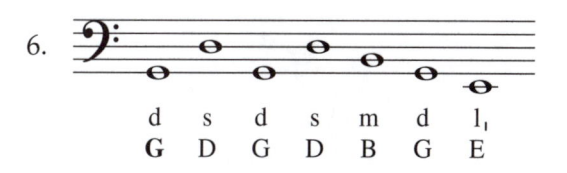

1.
m r d s, d s
B A G D G D

2.
s d r m s d r
D G A B D G A

3.
l, d s m r d
E G D B A G

4.
r d s, l, d m s
A G D E G B D

5.
s m d l, s, d
D B G E D G

6.
d s d s m d l,
G D G D B G E

21

DICTATION

Play the tracks one at a time. Each track will play the melody twice. Write the melodic pattern that you hear. Answers are on page 45.

PLAY CD TRACKS 35–40

1.
s₁ _ _ _ _ _ _
D _ _ _ _ _ _

2.
r _ _ _ _ _ _
A _ _ _ _ _ _

3.
m _ _ _ _ _ _
B _ _ _ _ _ _

4.
d _ _ _ _ _ _
G _ _ _ _ _ _

5.
l₁ _ _ _ _ _ _
E _ _ _ _ _ _

6.
m _ _ _ _ _ _
B _ _ _ _ _ _

CHAPTER 5

Sharps, Half Steps, and *ti* below *do*

NEW ELEMENT

An ACCIDENTAL is a symbol placed before a note that alters the pitch by raising or lowering it. A SHARP is an accidental that *raises* the pitch of a note.

A sharp is placed before the note that it alters and looks like this: ♯.

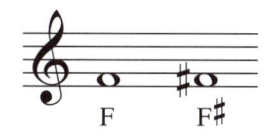

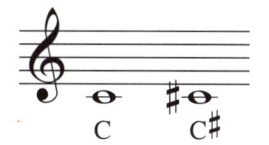

LISTENING

Track 41 plays the two examples above. In each case, the second note that you hear is slightly higher than the first.

PLAY CD TRACK 41

A sharp raises a pitch by a HALF STEP (or SEMITONE). If we look at a piano keyboard, we have a good visual aid to show that a half step is the distance from one key to the very next key, whether it is black or white.

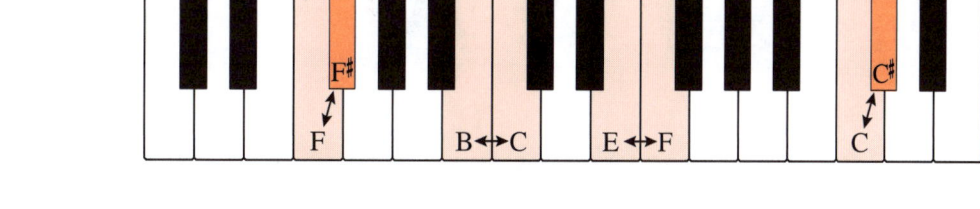

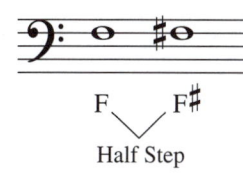

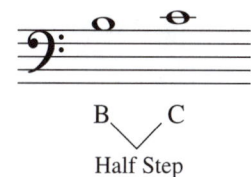

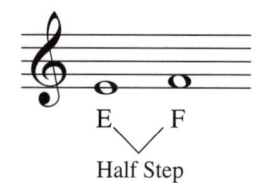

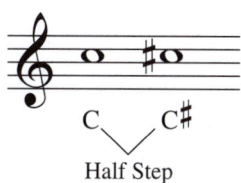

LISTENING

Beethoven's "Für Elise" begins with a series of half steps.

PLAY CD TRACK 42

NEW ELEMENT

Our new note is *ti* below *do*. The letter name is F♯ and is written in the first space on the treble staff or in the space below the bottom line on the bass staff.

Tonic Sol-fa Shorthand
t = *ti*

The interval from *ti* to *do* is a half step.

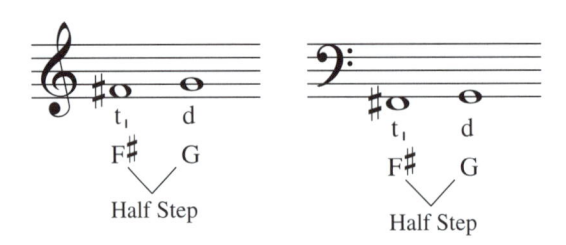

A sharp is written just before the note it alters. It also occupies the same line or space. Study the examples below.

To draw a sharp, simply write a number sign before the note, on the same line or space. Use the staves provided to practice drawing sharps.

Remember that familiar tunes can help with interval identification.

IDENTIFYING

Listen and identify the intervals in the following exercises, then write in the notes. The first one has been done for you. Answers are on page 45.

PLAY CD TRACK 43

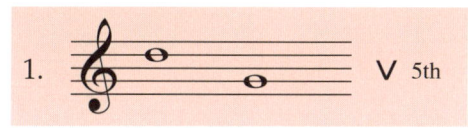

1. ✓ 5th
2. ___
3. ___
4. ___
5. ___
6. ___

MATCHING

Listen to the tracks one at a time and find the matching melodies below. Write the letter of the matching melody in the space provided. Answers are on page 45.

PLAY CD TRACK 44

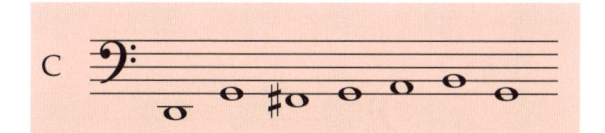

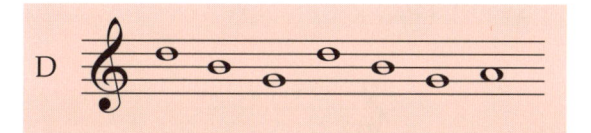

1. ___ 2. ___ 3. ___

4. ___ 5. ___ 6. ___

SIGHT-SINGING

Sing each exercise twice, once using tonic sol-fa, and once using letter names. When singing letter names, remember to say "Fis" for F#. Check accuracy on your instrument or pitch pipe.

When we come to a sharp while singing letter names, we add "is" (pronounced like "eese" in the word "geese") to the letter to indicate the sharp. For example, F♯ becomes Fis.

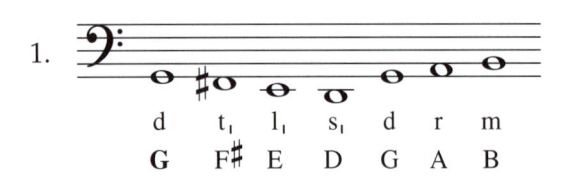

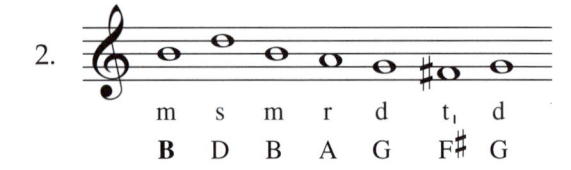

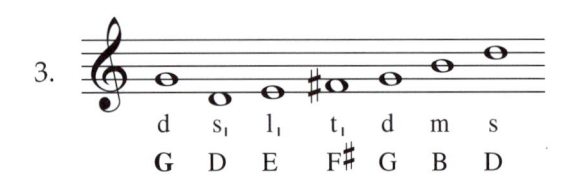

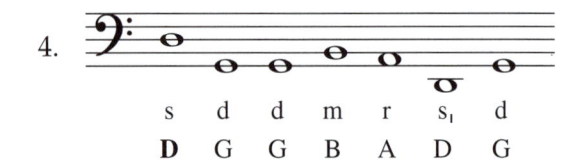

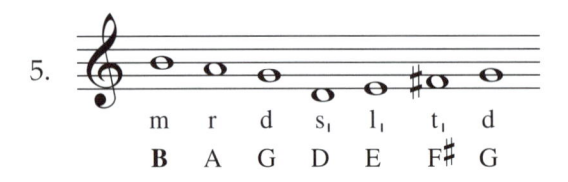

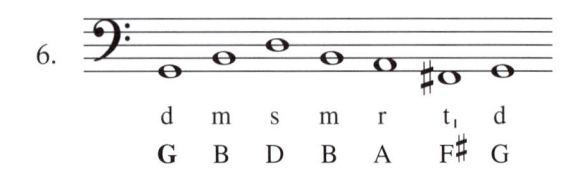

1.
d t₁ l₁ s₁ d r m
G F♯ E D G A B

2.
m s m r d t₁ d
B D B A G F♯ G

3.
d s₁ l₁ t₁ d m s
G D E F♯ G B D

4.
s d d m r s₁ d
D G G B A D G

5.
m r d s₁ l₁ t₁ d
B A G D E F♯ G

6.
d m s m r t₁ d
G B D B A F♯ G

DICTATION

Play the tracks one at a time. Each track will play the melody twice. Write the melodic pattern that you hear. Answers are on page 46.

PLAY CD TRACKS 45–50

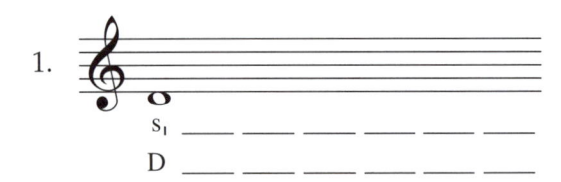

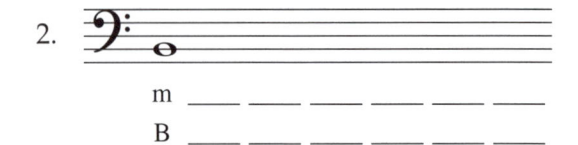

1. s₁ ___ ___ ___ ___ ___ ___
D ___ ___ ___ ___ ___ ___

2. m ___ ___ ___ ___ ___ ___
B ___ ___ ___ ___ ___ ___

3. d ___ ___ ___ ___ ___ ___
G ___ ___ ___ ___ ___ ___

4. m ___ ___ ___ ___ ___ ___
B ___ ___ ___ ___ ___ ___

5. s ___ ___ ___ ___ ___ ___
D ___ ___ ___ ___ ___ ___

6. d ___ ___ ___ ___ ___ ___
G ___ ___ ___ ___ ___ ___

CHAPTER 6

Moveable *do*, *do* above *do*, and the Octave

NEW ELEMENT

So far in our studies, *do* has been G. However, *do* is not always G. For example, in one piece of music, *do* may be C, and in another piece, *do* may be F. We call this system of tonic sol-fa **MOVEABLE DO**.

Study the examples below. Both show an interval of a 5th between *do* and *so*. In Example 1, *do* = G. In Example 2, *do* = C.

Example 1
- d = G
- s = D
- 5th

Example 2
- d = C
- s = G
- 5th

LISTENING

Track 51 plays the Examples 1 and 2 above, which demonstrate that the sound of a 5th above *do* is the same, even when *do* moves.

PLAY CD TRACK 51

*Note that both the tonic sol-fa names and the interval relationships remain the same, even when the starting pitch for **do** is different.*

LISTENING

Listen to the following examples to hear the interval of a 3rd between *do* and *la*. In Example 3, *do* = C. In example 4, *do* = G.

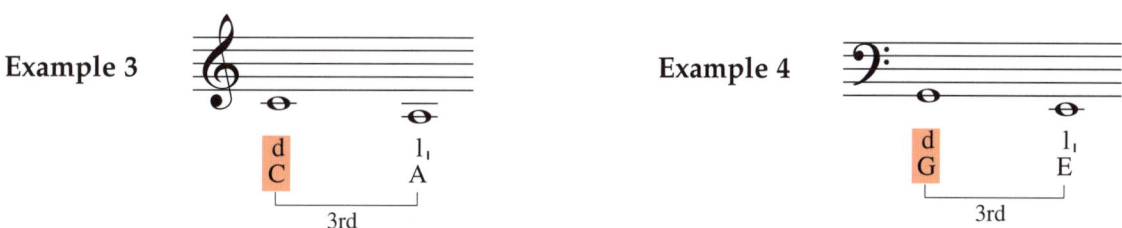

PLAY CD TRACK 52

Example 3
- d = C
- l₁ = A
- 3rd

Example 4
- d = G
- l₁ = E
- 3rd

Once again you will hear that the sound of a 3rd below **do** is the same, even when **do** moves.

LISTENING

Listen to "Twinkle, Twinkle, Little Star." Track 53 plays extended versions of Examples 5 and 6. In Example 5, *do* = F. In Example 6, *do* = C. As you will hear, the tune is exactly the same, even when the starting *do* is different.

PLAY CD TRACK 53

Example 5

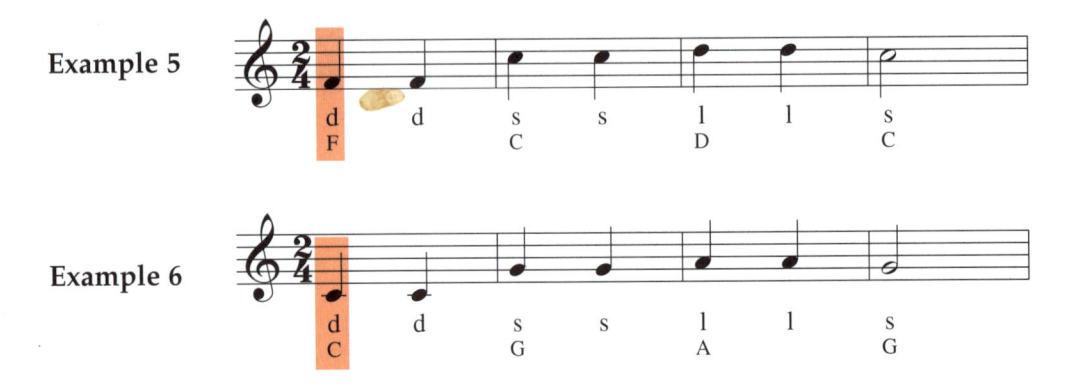

d   d   s   s   l   l   s
F   C   D   C

Example 6

d   d   s   s   l   l   s
C   G   A   G

NEW ELEMENT

Our new interval is the *do* above *do*. To indicate *do* above *do*, we use the upper index symbol.

Tonic Sol-fa Shorthand

d¹ = *do* above *do*

The interval from *do* to *do* is an 8th. This interval is also called an **OCTAVE**.

When *do* = G, the *do* an octave above it also has the letter name G, and is in the first space above the treble staff. In the bass clef, it is in the fourth space of the staff. Study the following examples.

d   d¹   d   d¹
G   G   G   G
  Octave   Octave

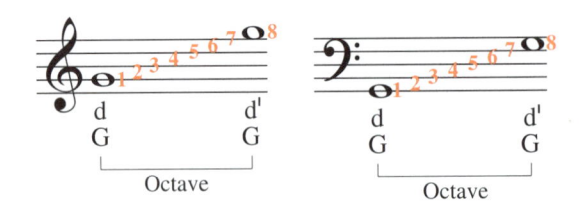

When *do* = C, the *do* an octave above it also has the letter name C, and is in the third space of the treble staff. When written in the bass clef, it is on the first ledger line above the staff. Study the following examples.

d   d¹   d   d¹
C   C   C   C

28

When *do* = F, the *do* an octave above it also has the letter name F, and is on the top line of the treble staff. When written in the bass clef, it is on the fourth line of the staff. Study the following examples.

LISTENING

Listen for the octave in the following melody. In Example 7, *do* = G. In Example 8, *do* = C.

PLAY CD TRACK 54

Example 7

Example 8

The song "Over the Rainbow" from the musical *The Wizard of Oz* also begins with an octave.

IDENTIFYING

Listen and identify the intervals in the following exercises, then write in the notes. Answers are on page 46.

PLAY CD TRACK 55

MATCHING

Listen to Track 56 and find the matching melodies below. Write the letter of the matching melody in the space provided. Answers are on page 46.

PLAY CD TRACK 56

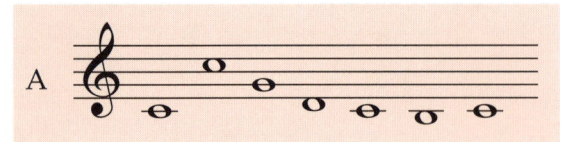

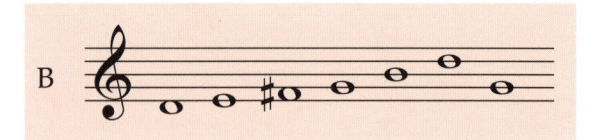

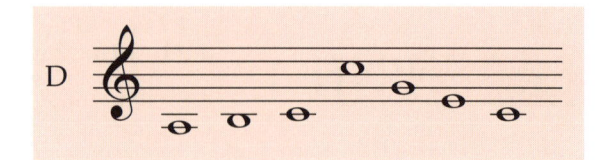

1. _____ 2. _____ 3. _____

4. _____ 5. _____ 6. _____

SIGHT-SINGING

Sing each exercise twice, once using tonic sol-fa and once using letter names. Check for accuracy on your instrument or pitch pipe.

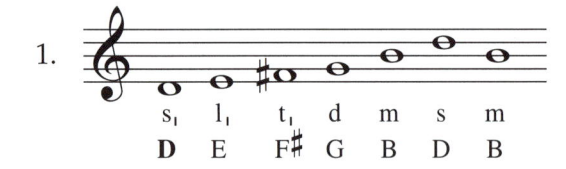

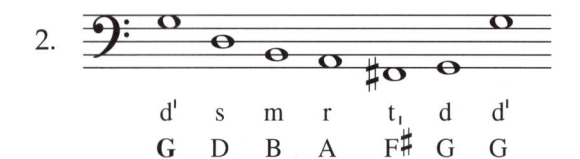

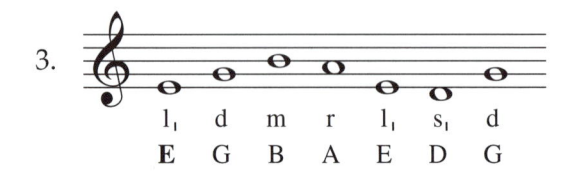

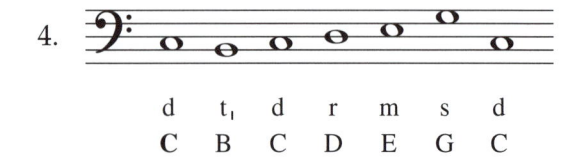

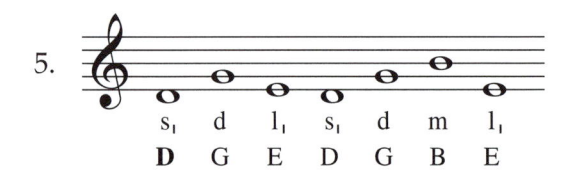

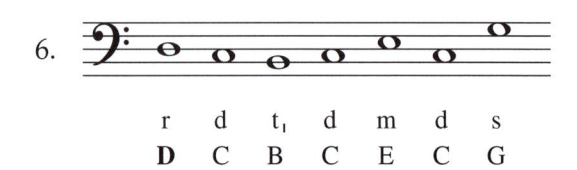

1. s₁ l₁ t₁ d m s m
    D   E   F# G B D B

2. d' s m r t₁ d d'
    G   D B A F# G G

3. l₁ d m r l₁ s₁ d
    E   G B A E   D   G

4. d   t₁ d r m s d
    C   B   C D E G C

5. s₁ d l₁ s₁ d m l₁
    D   G E   D   G B E

6. r d t₁ d m d s
    D C B   C E C G

30

DICTATION

Play the tracks one at a time. Each track will play the melody twice. Write the melodic pattern that you hear. Answers are on page 46.

PLAY CD TRACKS 57–62

1. d _ _ _ _ _ _
   G _ _ _ _ _ _

2. s _ _ _ _ _ _
   G _ _ _ _ _ _

3. m _ _ _ _ _ _
   E _ _ _ _ _ _

4. d _ _ _ _ _ _
   G _ _ _ _ _ _

5. s₁ _ _ _ _ _ _
   C _ _ _ _ _ _

6. d _ _ _ _ _ _
   G _ _ _ _ _ _

Until now, we have not used varied rhythms in our exercises and dictations. Rhythm has been introduced separately in the *Rhythm Without the Blues* series. However, it is important to begin to hear not only the melodic movement, but to hear rhythm patterns, as well.

In this chapter, we will be adding another set of exercises called **INTEGRATION**. In these exercises, you will be asked to notate the melody that you hear. Read the instructions carefully and study Exercise 1, which has been completed for you.

INTEGRATION

Play the tracks one at a time. Each track will play the melody twice. The starting tonic sol-fa is given. First, above the staff, write the rhythm you hear. Next, write the tonic sol-fa below the staff. Finally, fill in the complete dictation on the staff. The first exercise has been done for you. Answers are on page 46.

PLAY CD TRACKS 63–66

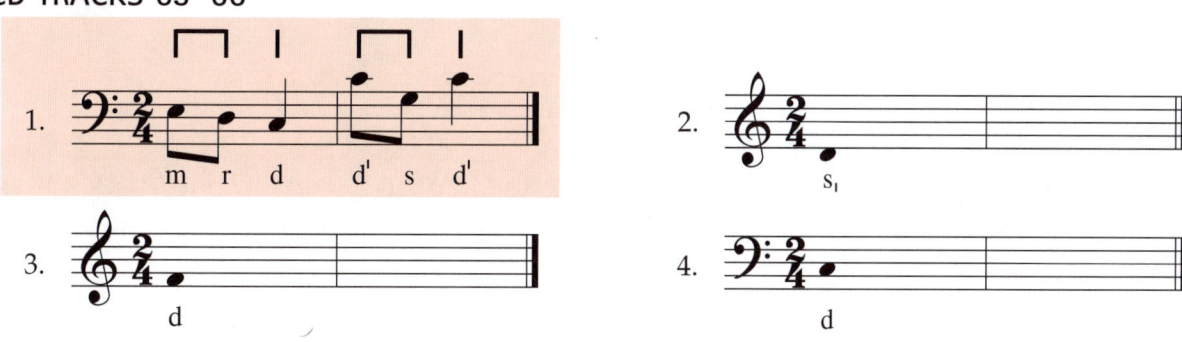

1. m r d d' s d'

2. s₁

3. d

4. d

*For more on rhythm, we recommend the companion series **Rhythm Without the Blues**, a comprehensive rhythm-training program. Using **Rhythm Without the Blues** in tandem with this ear-training series will greatly improve your success with the integration exercises.*

CHAPTER 7

Flats and *fa*

NEW ELEMENT

We have already been introduced to accidentals—symbols placed before a note that alter the pitch by raising or lowering it. We know that a sharp raises a note by a half step (semitone).

A **FLAT** is an accidental placed in front of a note that lowers a pitch by a half step.

A flat is placed before the note that it alters and looks like this: ♭.

LISTENING

Listen to the following examples. In each case, the second note that you hear is slightly lower than the first.

PLAY CD TRACK 67

A flat lowers a pitch by a half step (semitone). If we look at a piano keyboard, we have a good visual aid to show that a half step is the distance from one key to the very next key, whether it is black or white.

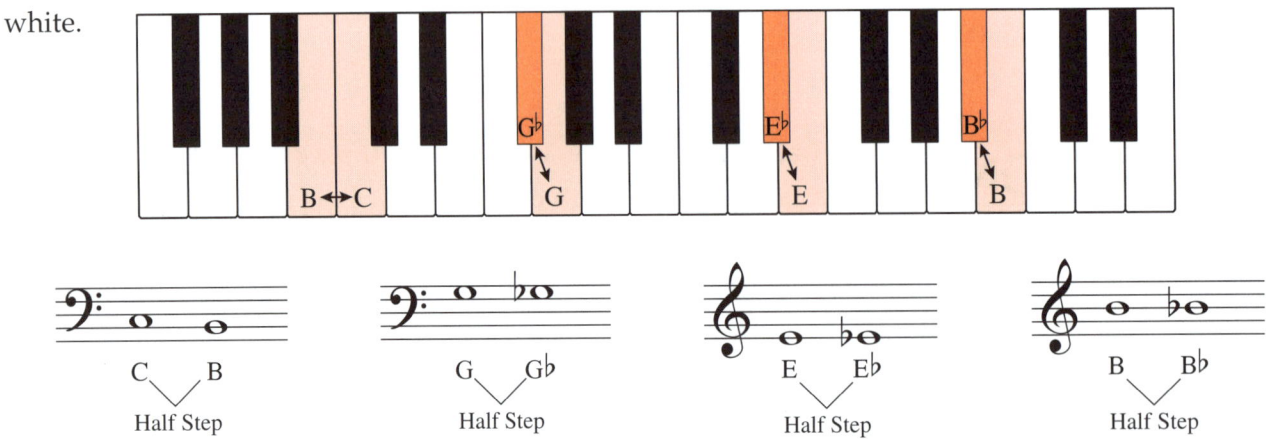

NEW ELEMENT

Our new note is *fa* above *do*. When *do* = G, *fa* is C and is written in the third space on the treble staff, or in the second space of the bass staff.

Tonic Sol-fa Shorthand

f = *fa*

When *do* = C, *fa* is F and is written in the first space of the treble staff or on the fourth line of the bass staff.

When *do* = F, *fa* is B♭ and is written on the third line of the treble staff or on the second line of the bass staff.

The interval from *do* to *fa* is called a 4th.

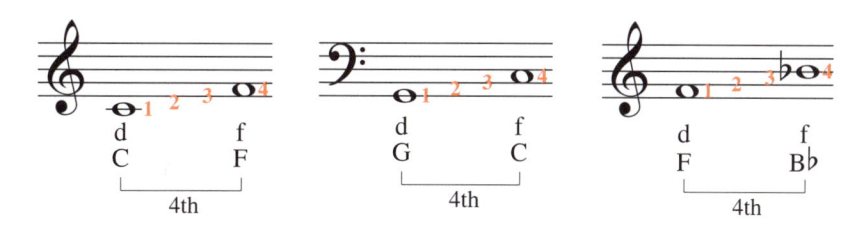

LISTENING Listen for the 4th in "Hark! The Herald Angels Sing."

PLAY CD TRACK 68

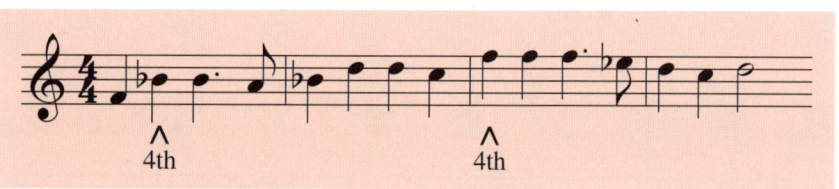

A flat is written just before the note it alters. It also occupies the same line or space. Study the following examples.

To make a flat sign, simply mark a vertical line and then draw half of a heart-shape on the right side of the vertical line. Place the flat sign before the note, on the same line or space as the note. Use the staves provided to practice drawing flats.

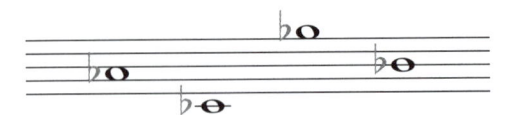

IDENTIFYING Listen and identify the intervals in the following exercises, then write in the notes. Answers are on page 46.

PLAY CD TRACK 69

1.

2.

3.

4.

5.

6.

34

MATCHING

Listen to Track 70 and find the matching melodies below. Write the letter of the matching melody in the space provided. Answers are on page 46.

PLAY CD TRACK 70

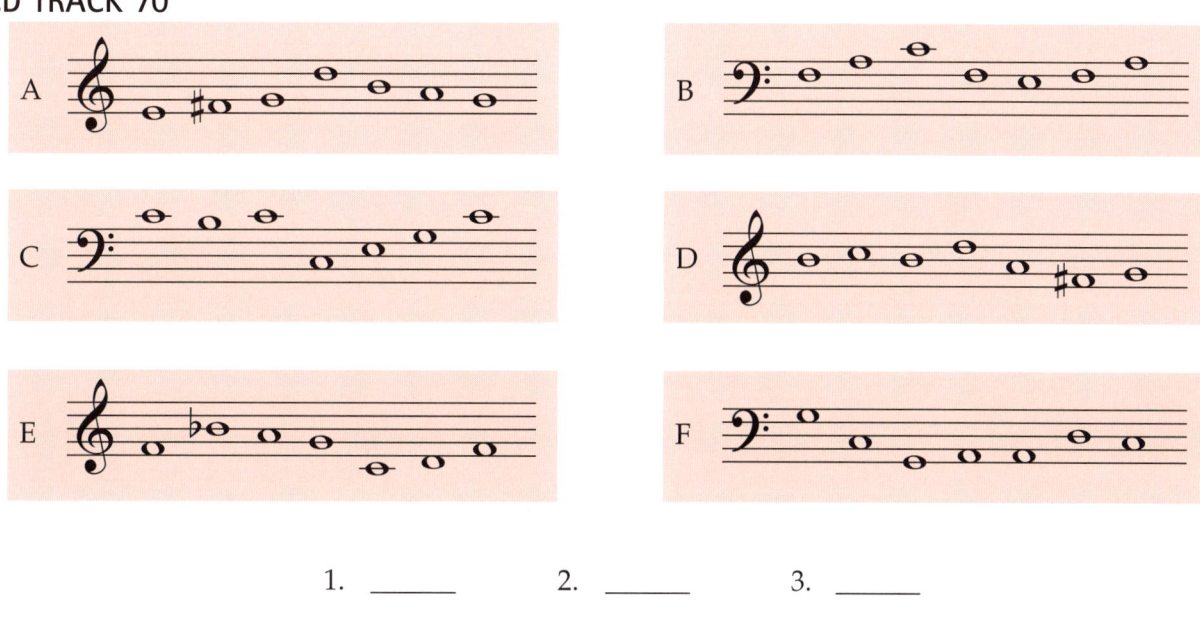

A, B, C, D, E, F (music staves)

1. _____ 2. _____ 3. _____

4. _____ 5. _____ 6. _____

When we come to a flat while singing letter names, we add "es" (pronounced like "ess" in the name "Bess") to the letter to indicate the flat. For example, B♭ becomes "Bes."

SIGHT-SINGING

Sing each exercise twice, once using tonic sol-fa and once using letter names. Check for accuracy on your keyboard or pitch pipe.

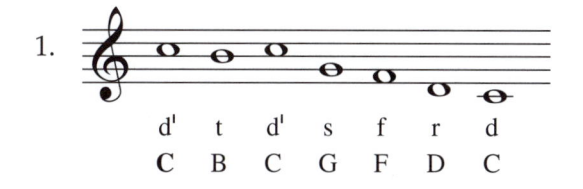

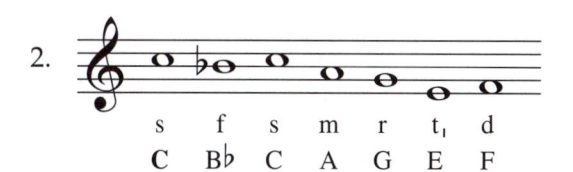

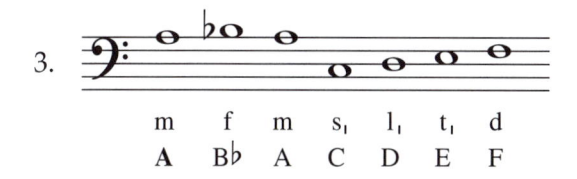

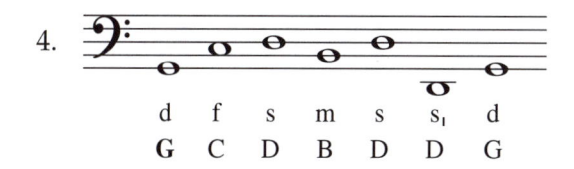

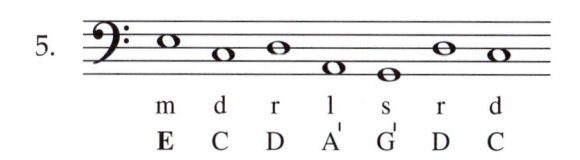

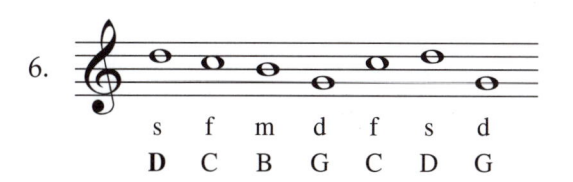

1. d¹ t   d¹ s   f   r   d
    C   B   C   G   F   D   C

2. s   f   s   m   r   t₁ d
    C   B♭ C   A   G   E   F

3. m   f   m   s₁ l₁ t₁ d
    A   B♭ A   C   D   E   F

4. d   f   s   m   s   s₁ d
    G   C   D   B   D   D   G

5. m   d   r   l   s   r   d
    E   C   D   A¹ G¹ D   C

6. s   f   m   d   f   s   d
    D   C   B   G   C   S   D

35

DICTATION

Play the tracks one at a time. Each track will play the melody twice. Write the melodic pattern that you hear. Answers are on page 47.

PLAY CD TRACKS 71–76

1. s₁ _ _ _ _ _ _
   C _ _ _ _ _ _

2. m _ _ _ _ _ _
   B _ _ _ _ _ _

3. r _ _ _ _ _ _
   A _ _ _ _ _ _

4. d _ _ _ _ _ _
   F _ _ _ _ _ _

5. d¹ _ _ _ _ _ _
   C _ _ _ _ _ _

6. d _ _ _ _ _ _
   C _ _ _ _ _ _

INTEGRATION

Play the tracks one at a time. Each track will play the melody twice. The starting tonic sol-fa is given. First, above the staff, write the rhythm you hear. Next, write the tonic sol-fa below the staff. Finally, fill in the complete dictation on the staff. The first exercise has been done for you. Answers are on page 47 (full melodies only).

PLAY CD TRACKS 77–80

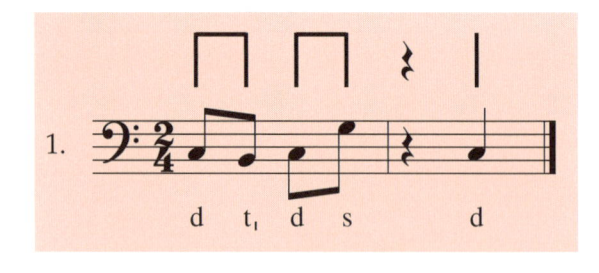

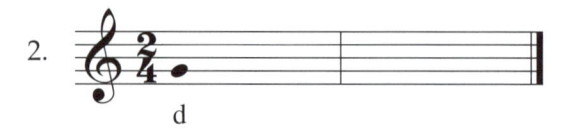

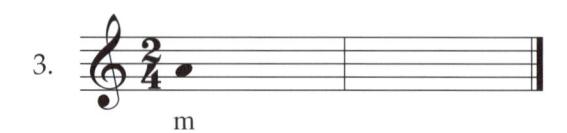

1. d t₁ d s   d

2. d

3. m

4. s₁

36

CHAPTER 8

la and the 6th

NEW ELEMENT — Our new note is *la* above *do*. When *do* = G, *la* is E and is written in the top space of the treble staff or the third space of the bass staff.

Tonic Sol-fa Shorthand
l = *la*

l
E

l
E

When *do* = C, *la* is A and is written in the second space of the treble staff or the top line of the bass staff.

l
A

l
A

When *do* = F, *la* is D and is written on the fourth line of the treble staff or the third line of the bass staff.

l
D

l
D

The interval from *do* to *la* is called a **6th**.

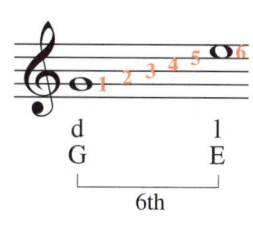

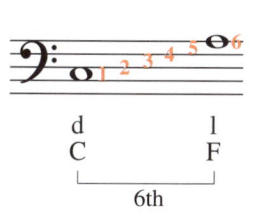

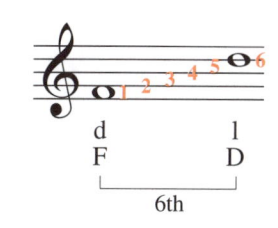

d	l
G	E

6th

d	l
C	F

6th

d	l
F	D

6th

37

LISTENING

Listen for the 6th in "My Bonny Lies Over the Ocean."

PLAY CD TRACK 81

IDENTIFYING

Listen and identify the intervals in the following exercises, then write in the notes. Answers are on page 47.

PLAY CD TRACK 82

1.
2.
3.
4.
5.
6.

MATCHING

Listen to Track 83 and find the matching melodies below. Write the letter of the matching melody in the space provided. Answers are on page 47.

PLAY CD TRACK 83

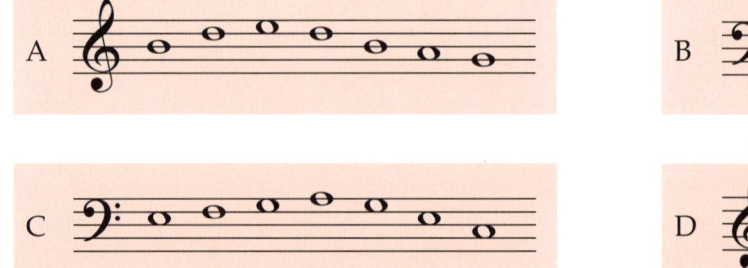

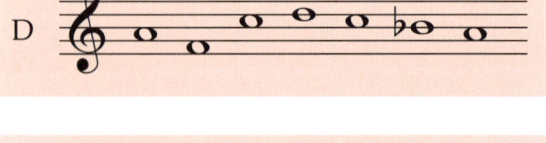

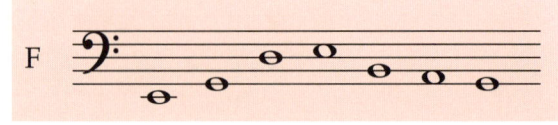

A
B
C
D
E
F

1. _____   2. _____   3. _____

4. _____   5. _____   6. _____

SIGHT-SINGING

Sing each exercise twice, once using tonic sol-fa and once using letter names. Check for accuracy on your instrument or pitch pipe.

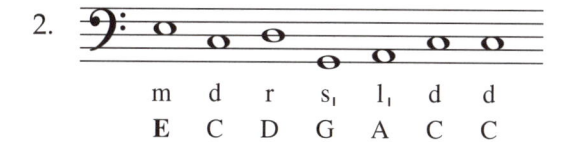

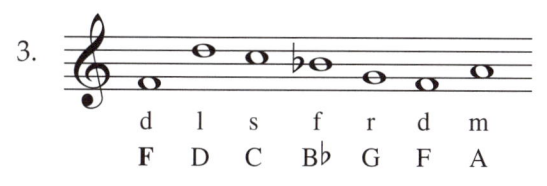

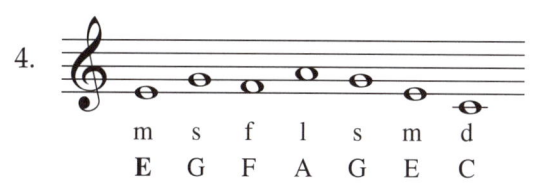

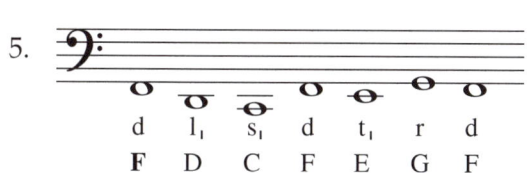

1. d s l s f r d
   G D E D C A G

2. m d r s, l, d d
   E C D G A C C

3. d l s f r d m
   F D C B♭ G F A

4. m s f l s m d
   E G F A G E C

5. d l, s, d t, r d
   F D C F E G F

6. d l s f s t, d
   G E D C D F♯ G

DICTATION

Play the tracks one at a time. Each track will play the melody twice. Write the melodic pattern that you hear. Answers are on page 47.

PLAY CD TRACKS 84–89

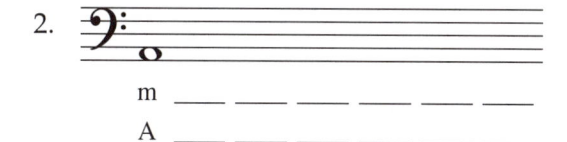

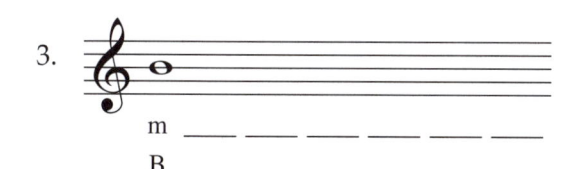

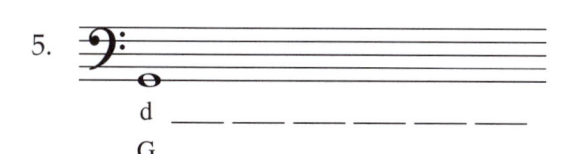

1. d ___ ___ ___ ___ ___ ___
   C ___ ___ ___ ___ ___ ___

2. m ___ ___ ___ ___ ___ ___
   A ___ ___ ___ ___ ___ ___

3. m ___ ___ ___ ___ ___ ___
   B ___ ___ ___ ___ ___ ___

4. s ___ ___ ___ ___ ___ ___
   C ___ ___ ___ ___ ___ ___

5. d ___ ___ ___ ___ ___ ___
   G ___ ___ ___ ___ ___ ___

6. d ___ ___ ___ ___ ___ ___
   C ___ ___ ___ ___ ___ ___

INTEGRATION

Play the tracks one at a time. Each track will play the melody twice. Write the melody that you hear. Answers are on page 47.

PLAY CD TRACKS 90–93

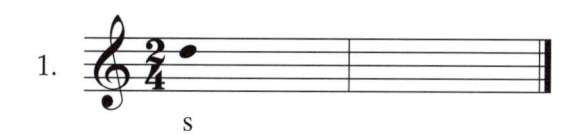

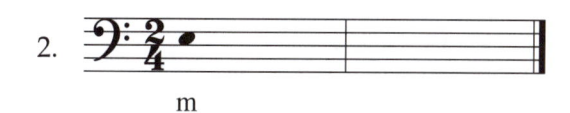

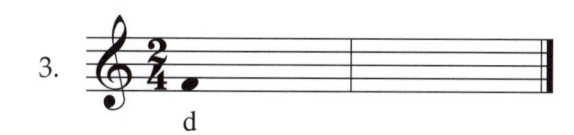

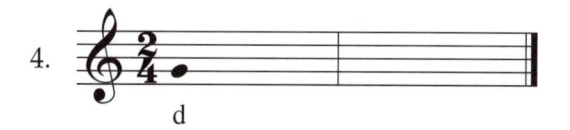

1. s

2. m

3. d

4. d

REVIEW TEST

The test consists of five parts, Review Questions, Matching, Sight-Singing, Dictation, and Integration. Total possible points are listed to the left of each section heading.

The entire test is worth a total of 113 points. Answers are on page 48.

REVIEW QUESTIONS   Each answer is worth one point.

POINTS: 17

1. *Do* must always be on the same line or space.   T   F

2. *Fixed Do* is the name of the tonic sol-fa system in which *do* may exist on different lines and spaces.   T   F

3. A ledger line extends the staff above or below the existing staff.   T   F

4. Only three ledger lines may be used in a given piece of music.   T   F

5. Draw a sharp: _____

6. A sharp slightly raises the pitch of the note it is placed beside.   T   F

7. Accidentals are placed to the right of the notes they alter.   T   F

8. Draw a flat: _____

9. Lower pitches are notated on the _____ staff.

In the following exercises, fill in the required intervals along with the corresponding tonic sol-fa.

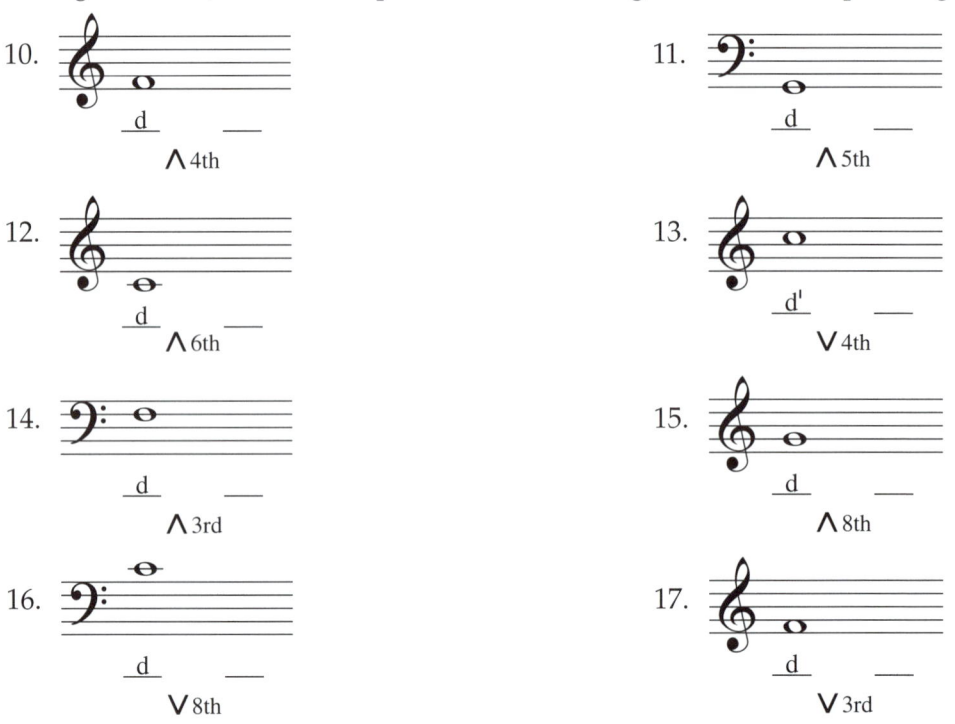

10. d ___ ∧ 4th

11. d ___ ∧ 5th

12. d ___ ∧ 6th

13. d' ___ ∨ 4th

14. d ___ ∧ 3rd

15. d ___ ∧ 8th

16. d ___ ∨ 8th

17. d ___ ∨ 3rd

Score: _____ out of 17

You should score a total of at least 14 out of 17 before proceeding to the next section.

40

POINTS 6

MATCHING

Listen to Track 94 and find the matching melodies below. Write the letter of the matching melody in the space provided. Each answer is worth 1 point, for a total of 6 points.

🎵 PLAY CD TRACK 94

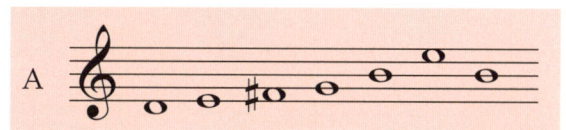

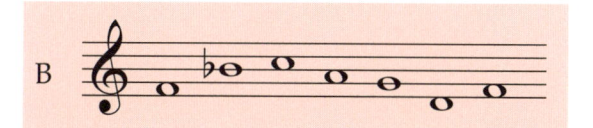

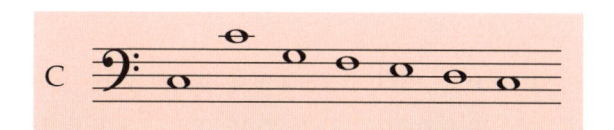

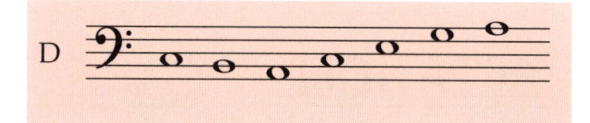

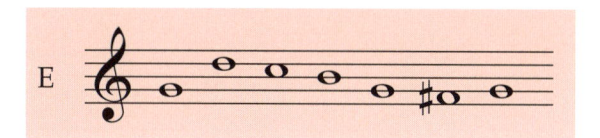

1. _____   2. _____   3. _____

4. _____   5. _____   6. _____

Score: _____ out of 6

POINTS 6

SIGHT-SINGING

Sing each exercise twice, once using tonic sol-fa and once using letter names. Check for accuracy on your keyboard or pitch pipe. Each correctly-sung exercise is worth 1 point for a total of 6 points.

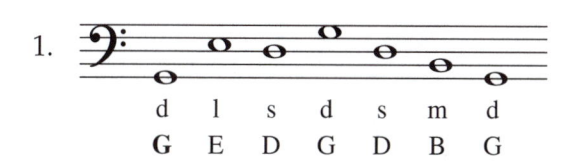

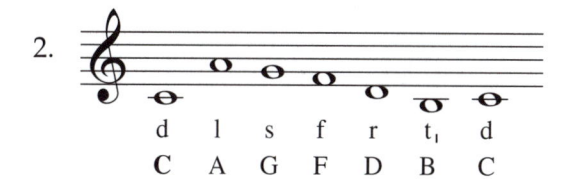

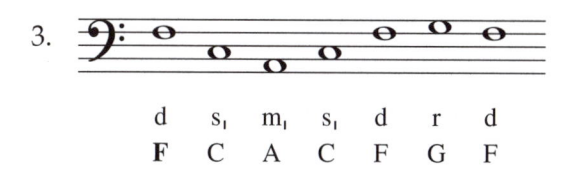

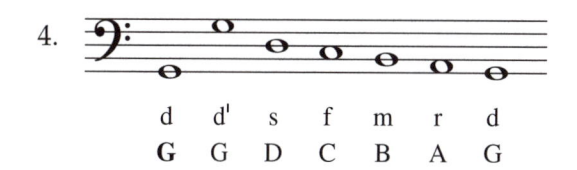

1. d l s d s m d
    G E D G D B G

2. d l s f r t₁ d
    C A G F D B C

3. d s₁ m₁ s₁ d r d
    F C A C F G F

4. d d' s f m r d
    G G D C B A G

41

5.

d f r l, s, r d
F B♭ G D C G F

6.

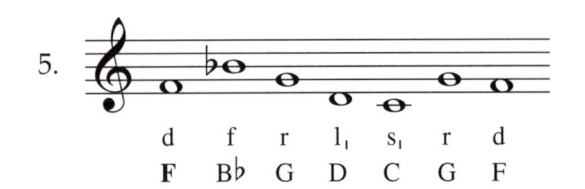

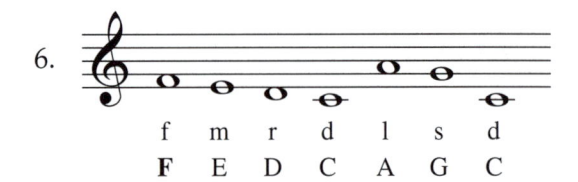

f m r d l s d
F E D C A G C

Ask your teacher to check your accuracy and assign a score for this part of the review.

Score: _____ out of 6

POINTS 48

DICTATION

Track 95 will play eight different melodies. Each melody will be played twice. Listen and write the melodic patterns you hear. Each exercise is worth 6 points, for a total of 48 points.

PLAY CD TRACK 95

1.

d ___ ___ ___ ___ ___
G ___ ___ ___ ___ ___

2.

m ___ ___ ___ ___ ___
A ___ ___ ___ ___ ___

3.

r ___ ___ ___ ___ ___
D ___ ___ ___ ___ ___

4.

r ___ ___ ___ ___ ___
G ___ ___ ___ ___ ___

5.

s, ___ ___ ___ ___ ___
C ___ ___ ___ ___ ___

6.

d ___ ___ ___ ___ ___
G ___ ___ ___ ___ ___

7.

m ___ ___ ___ ___ ___
A ___ ___ ___ ___ ___

8.

r ___ ___ ___ ___ ___
D ___ ___ ___ ___ ___

Score: _____ out of 48

POINTS 36

INTEGRATION

Track 96 will play six different melodies. Each melody will be played twice. Write the melody that you hear. Total points for each answer are indicated before each question.

PLAY CD TRACK 96

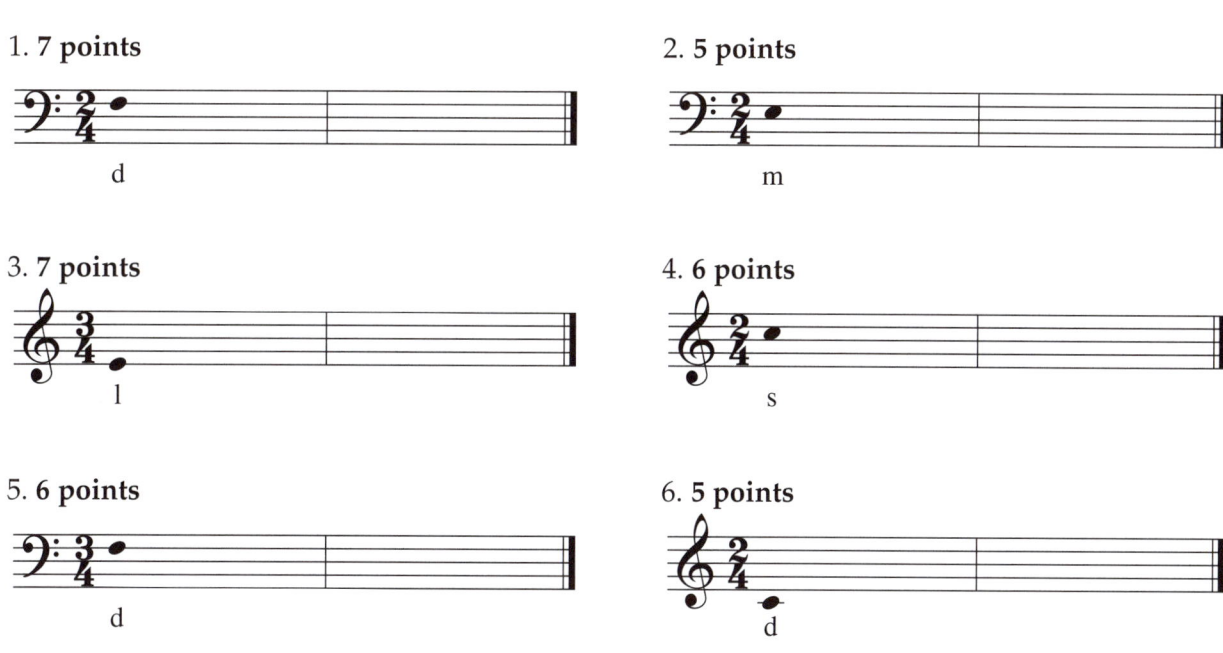

1. 7 points

d

2. 5 points

m

3. 7 points

l

4. 6 points

s

5. 6 points

d

6. 5 points

d

Score: _____ out of 36

TOTAL SCORE_____OUT OF 113

If your score is 102 or better, Congratulations! You may now proceed to

EAR WITHOUT FEAR VOLUME 3

If your score was 101 or less, you should review any elements that gave you difficulty before continuing.

43

Answers

CHAPTER 1

LISTENING:

2. ˅ ˄˄ ˅ ˅˅ 
   d m r d
   A G B A G

3. — ˄˄ ˄ ˅˅
   d r m d
   G G A B G

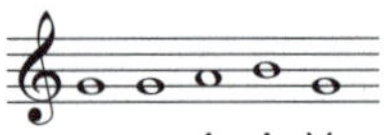

4. ˅˅ ˄˄ ˅˅ ˄
   d m d r
   B G B G A

MATCHING:

1. F
2. A
3. D
4. C
5. B
6. E

DICTATION:

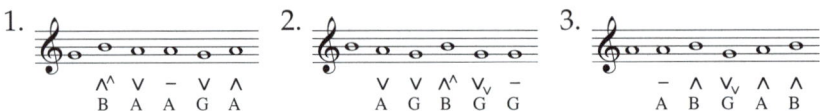

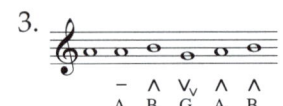

1. ˄˄ ˅ — ˅ ˄
   B A A G A

2. ˅ ˅ ˄˄ ˅˅ —
   A G B G G

3. — ˄ ˅˅ ˄ ˄
   A B G A B

4. ˄ ˅ ˅ ˄˄ ˅˅
   B A G B G

5. ˄˄ ˅˅ ˄ ˅ —
   B G A G G

6. ˅˅ — ˄ ˄ ˅
   G G A B A

CHAPTER 2

IDENTIFYING:

2. ˄ 2nd
3. ˅ 3rd
4. ˄ 2nd
5. ˄ 3rd

IDENTIFYING:

2. ˅ 2nd
3. ˅ 4th
4. ˅ 3rd

MATCHING:

1. D
2. B
3. E
4. C
5. F
6. A

DICTATION:

1. m r d s₁ d
   B A G D G

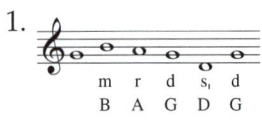

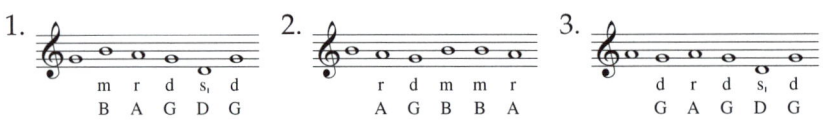

2. r d m m r
   A G B B A

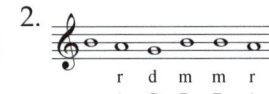

3. d r d s₁ d
   G A G D G

4. d r m d d
   G A B G G

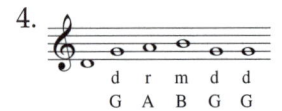

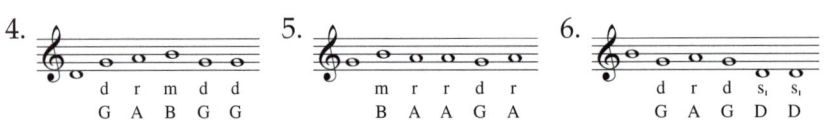

5. m r r d r
   B A A G A

6. d r d s₁ s₁
   G A G D D

44

CHAPTER 3

IDENTIFYING:

2. ∧ 4th   3. ∧ 2nd   4. ∧ 3rd

MATCHING:

1. D   2. F   3. C
4. A   5. E   6. B

DICTATION:

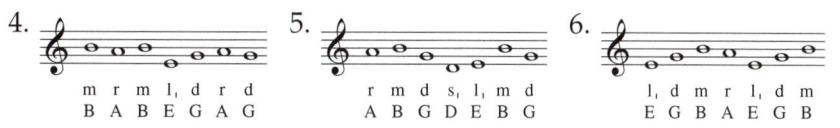

1. d l, d m r s, d
   G E G B A D G

2. s, l, s, l, d m r
   D E D E G B A

3. l, s d l, m r d
   E D G E B A G

4. m r m l, d r d
   B A B E G A G

5. r m d s, l, m d
   A B G D E B G

6. l, d m r l, d m
   E G B A E G B

CHAPTER 4

IDENTIFYING:

2. ∧ 5th   3. ∧ 3rd   4. ∨ 3rd
5. ∨ 5th   6. ∧ 3rd

MATCHING:

1. D   2. C   3. E
4. B   5. F   6. A

DICTATION:

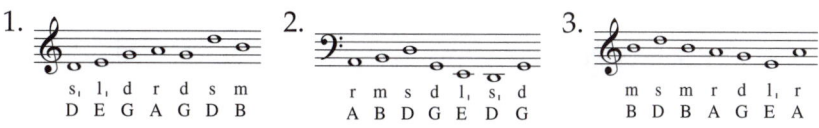

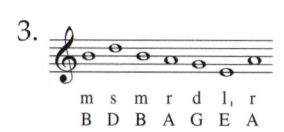

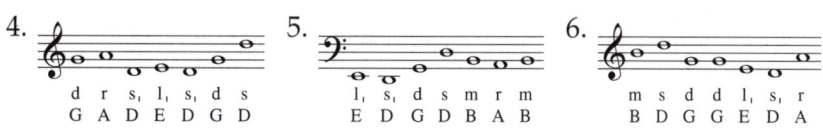

1. s, l, d r d s m
   D E G A G D B

2. r m s d l, s, d
   A B D G E D G

3. m s m r d l, r
   B D B A G E A

4. d r s, l, s d s
   G A D E D G D

5. l, s, d s m r m
   E D G D B A B

6. m s d d l, s, r
   B D G G E D A

CHAPTER 5

IDENTIFYING:

2. ∧ 3rd   3. ∨ 4th   4. ∧ 2nd
5. ∨ 2nd   6. ∧ 5th

MATCHING:

1. F   2. A   3. C
4. E   5. D   6. B

45

DICTATION:

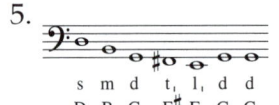

1. s, d t, d r m d
   D G F# G A B G

2. m s m r d t, d
   B D B A G F# G

3. d m l, r d t, d
   G B E A G F# G

4. m s s m r d s,
   B D D B A G D

5. s m d t, l, d d
   D B G F# E G G

6. d s m d s, t, d
   G D B G D F# G

CHAPTER 6

IDENTIFYING:

1. ∧ 8th
2. ∧ 8th
3. ∨ 4th
4. ∨ 2nd
5. ∨ 5th
6. ∧ 8th

MATCHING:

1. E   2. C   3. D
4. A   5. B   6. F

DICTATION:

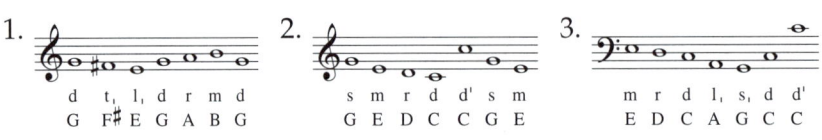

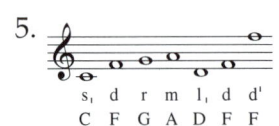

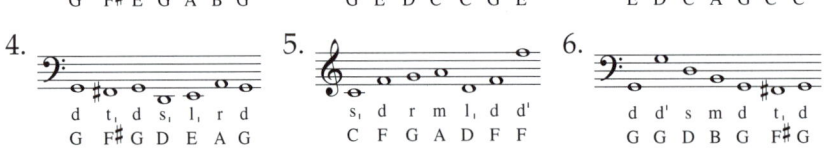

1. d t, l, d r m d
   G F# E G A B G

2. s m r d d' s m
   G E D C C G E

3. m r d l, s, d d'
   E D C A G C C

4. d t, d s, l, r d
   G F# G D E A G

5. s, d r m l, d d'
   C F G A D F F

6. d d' s m d t, d
   G G D B G F# G

INTEGRATION:

2. 3. 4.

CHAPTER 7

IDENTIFYING:

1. ∧ 4th
2. ∨ 8th
3. ∧ 4th
4. ∧ 5th
5. ∨ 3rd
6. ∨ 4th

MATCHING:

1. E   2. C   3. F
4. B   5. A   6. D

DICTATION:

1. s, d m s f r d
   C F A C B♭ G F

2. m s d t, d m s
   B D G F# G B D

3. r m d s l, s, r
   A B G D E D A

4. d m f r m s d
   F A B♭ G A C F

5. d' t d' d s f r
   C B C C G F D

6. d f m s s t, d
   C F E G G B C

INTEGRATION:

2. 3. 4.

CHAPTER 8

IDENTIFYING:

1. ∧ 6th
2. ∨ 5th
3. ∨ 6th
4. ∧ 3rd
5. ∧ 4th
6. ∧ 2nd

MATCHING:

1. E   2. C   3. B
4. A   5. F   6. D

DICTATION:

1. d l d r m s d
   C A C D E G C

2. m f s m r d r
   A B♭ C A G F G

3. m d s, d r m f
   B G D G A B C

4. s l s f m d s,
   C D C B♭ A F C

5. d l, d m f r d
   G E G B C A G

6. d s l f m r d
   C G A F E D C

INTEGRATION:

1. 2. 3. 4.

47

REVIEW TEST

QUESTIONS:

1. F
2. F
3. T
4. F
5. ♯
6. T
7. F
8. ♭
9. bass
10. d f
11. d s
12. d l
13. d' s
14. d m
15. d d'
16. d d,
17. d l,

MATCHING:

1. B
2. A
3. F
4. D
5. C
6. E

DICTATION:

1. d t, l, s, d s m
   G F♯ E D G D B
2. m f m r d t, d
   A B♭ A G F E F
3. r s f m d s, d
   D G F E C G C
4. r t, d m f m d
   G E F A B♭ A F
5. s, l, s, d m f s
   C D C F A B♭ C
6. d s f r s, l, d
   G D C A D E G
7. m r m s d t, d
   A G A C F E F
8. r s f r d s m
   D G F D C G E

INTEGRATION:

1.
2.
3.
4.
5.
6.